"People the world over come to June to find God's truth for today's problems. Her amazing insights have helped me personally through the difficult issues of forgiveness. I know they will help you."

—**Debbie Brunson**
Author, speaker, and colleague
in ministry to pastor's wives

"Page by page, June walks you through the step-by-step process to forgive…yes, even the 'unforgivable.' If you want your days ahead to be better than the days gone by, this is a must-read for you."

—**Dr. Tony Evans**
Senior Pastor, Oak Cliff Bible Fellowship
President, The Urban Alternative

"True forgiveness is possible, no matter how much you've been hurt. June's personal journey is proof!"

—**Suellen Roberts**
Founder and President,
Christian Women in Media Association

"Those of us who have had to forgive the unforgivable will find tremendous hope in healing. She speaks from the heart with truth, directly to your broken soul."

—**Stephen Arterburn**
Founder, New Life Ministries and
author of *Healing as a Choice*

"June has practiced what she preaches! She knows the forgiveness process because she's had to go through it. Her journey brings credibility to what she shares and you will love the grace, the support, and the direction you receive when you put *How to Forgive…When You Don't Feel Like It* into practice. It works!"

—**Dave Carder**
Author, *Torn Asunder: Recovering from an Extramarital Affair*

How to
FORGIVE...
When You Don't Feel Like It

JUNE HUNT

HARVEST HOUSE PUBLISHERS
EUGENE, OREGON

HOW TO FORGIVE...WHEN YOU DON'T FEEL LIKE IT
Copyright © 2007 by Hope for the Heart, Inc.
Published by Harvest House Publishers
Eugene, Oregon 97402
www.harvesthousepublishers.com

ISBN 978-0-7369-5589-8 (pbk.)
ISBN 978-0-7369-5590-4 (eBook)

Library of Congress Cataloging-in-Publication Data
Hunt, June.
How to forgive—when you don't feel like it / June Hunt.
   p. cm.
ISBN 978-0-7369-2148-0
1. Forgiveness—Religious aspects—Christianity. I. Title.
BV4647.F55H86 2007
234'.5—dc22

                                                         2007007023

≈

This book is dedicated to my forever friend, Barbara…

to the first friend willing to extend full forgiveness to me…

to my "grace friend" who was willing to look beyond my fault

and see my need. Thank you for allowing God to use your

forgiving heart to be a part of my emotional and spiritual

healing. You consistently give me hope for my heart.

≈

Acknowledgments

I have the privilege of working with what I believe is the greatest ministry team on earth—the dedicated staff and volunteers of Hope for the Heart. Thank you for your faithful prayers and support.

With heartfelt appreciation to:

—Carolyn White, Elizabeth Gaston, Jill Prohaska, and Barbara Spruill, who worked countless hours to fine-tune the manuscript

—Keith Wall, who converted a mountain of interview notes, audio archives, and written materials into a wonderful first draft

—Mark Overstreet, Brad Ray, and Jeanne Sloan, who helped me think about rocks in a new way!

—Connie Steindorf, Bea Garner, and Titus O'Bryant, whose behind-the-scenes support work was invaluable

—Steve Miller, my Harvest House editor, whose deft touch graces these pages, and

—Kay Deakins (who deserves a medal) for keeping the rest of us on task during this entire process.

Finally, I give highest praise to my Lord and Master, Jesus Christ, for not giving up on me. His forgiveness is why I have a story to tell about the lifechanging freedom of true forgiveness.

On a Personal Note

Throughout the writing of this book, I have repeatedly thought about those whom I have hurt in the past...and my heart has grieved. I am without excuse. I cannot help but ask forgiveness from the deepest part of my heart. Many times I have prayed, "Lord, may I see my sin as You see it—may I hate my sin as You hate it." He has painfully answered my prayer. His cleansing love has enabled me to "walk in the light as He Himself is in the light" (1 John 1:7 NASB).

Contents

THE STRUGGLE
TO FORGIVE

RESENTMENT. RAGE. RETALIATION. Ever struggled with forgiveness? Ever thought it was impossible? Ever knew you *oughta* but didn't *wanna*? I believe the majority of the world's population is struggling with forgiveness—right now! If you are human (which you are) and if you are reading this book (which you are), you have been hurt—deeply and profoundly—and have faced the formidable foe of *un*forgiveness.

Each weeknight, I host a two-hour call-in counseling program—*Hope in the Night*—during which people across America pour out their hearts on live radio. I'm constantly amazed at their candor and profoundly touched by their pain.

I'm also grieved over the steady stream of people personally wronged and mistreated by others—from their own family to their church family...from casual acquaintances to close neighbors...from complete strangers to "best friends."

My heart goes out to the hurting—to those who just want their pain to stop and want to have hope again.

After more than a decade of hearing hundreds of heartrending stories, I come to the challenge of forgiveness with tremendous compassion. I don't want those who are hurting to be further hurt by living with *embedded bitterness*—simply because they don't grasp the true meaning of forgiveness...or they don't know the "how to's" of forgiveness.

And I come to this topic with more than compassion. I come with experience, having wrestled for years with unforgiveness. Indeed, I have felt its heavy weight. So for me, forgiveness is not merely a theoretical premise...or just a theological concept. Forgiveness is a real-world, nitty-gritty matter of the soul.

Forgiveness is a *decision*—an act of the will that, when done right, results in true freedom. It is a process—often misunderstood. It took me a long time to learn the *why* of forgiveness and even longer to *live out* the heart of forgiveness. The call of God in Colossians 3:13 has been the catalyst for my journey: "Bear with each other and forgive whatever grievances you may have against one another. Forgive as the Lord forgave you."

Through vivid illustrations and riveting real-life experiences, I want to connect you with others who have suffered greatly and forgiven much—some who thought they could never find peace because of the depth of their pain. And I want to point you to the One who has been offended the most and has forgiven the most... *Jesus*. He knows your pain, He knows your need, and He knows how to empower you to forgive—even when you feel it's impossible.

Through these pages, my prayer is twofold: (1) that you will learn how to get rid of the boulders of bitterness holding you back—those heavy rocks of resentment—and (2) that you will experience the freedom of forgiveness—a freedom only possible when you learn how to forgive...even when you don't feel like it.

1

"STICKS AND STONES MAY BREAK MY BONES..."

Words Can Break My Heart

IN MY GROWING-UP YEARS, I remember hearing many catchy sayings that made a lot of sense, such as, "People who live in glass houses shouldn't throw stones," and "A rolling stone gathers no moss."

Another popular adage is "Sticks and stones may break my bones, but words will never hurt me." What I say in response is, "Wrong, wrong, wrong!" We all know that words *can* break our hearts. The Bible puts it this way: "The tongue has the power of life and death, and those who love it will eat its fruit."[1]

Words can kill a relationship. Words can murder our motivation and inspiration. This truth was recently driven home to me when I was leading a conference in Indiana.

≈

"How many of you have *really* struggled with forgiveness? You've had a huge struggle forgiving someone who has hurt you deeply?"

Immediately hands go up...about one-fourth of the audience. Quickly I scan those with raised hands, looking for someone physically fit.

My question comes at the beginning of my talk on forgiveness, but it isn't until the final 15 minutes that I point to the thirtyish-year-old man.

"Sir, I need some help. Would you be willing to join me on the platform?" Surprised, he nods with a smile and saunters up to the stage. Now we both stand next to a table that has a mound of rocks. "Would you share your name and something about yourself?"

"My name is Rick. I'm an accountant, and my hobby is running. When I'm not at work, I'm usually running because I plan to enter a marathon this year."

"That's great, Rick! And thanks for being willing to help."

Reaching over to a small table, I pick up a large gray meat hook, more than two feet long, and a burlap bag. The top of the hook is able to fit around a person's neck like a horseshoe. A straight shaft extends down a couple feet then arches back up, like a very large fishhook with a sharp point.

"Here you go, Rick. Slip this meat hook carefully around your neck." His eyes open wide—the hook looks ominous. He gives me a wary glance. Some people in the audience groan (probably just glad they weren't picked!). Slowly, cautiously, Rick slides the top of the hook around his neck. The shaft of the hook reached down his chest to waist level, and the pointed tip was in front of him. I push the top of the burlap bag over the tip of the hook.

"Rick, at the beginning, when I asked if anyone had struggled with forgiveness, I noticed you raised your hand."

"That's right."

"What has been so hard to forgive? Would you tell me what happened?"

At this point I reach over to the mound of rocks, knowing that every time Rick mentions an offense, I will drop a rock or a small boulder into the burlap bag. Each rock represents a wrong someone has committed against him—a wound he is carrying.

Rick begins by going back to his childhood. It doesn't take long for us to learn that all his "rocks" come from the same source—growing up with a harsh, sometimes tyrannical father who was unaffectionate and inflexible. As Rick focuses on his father and the wrongs suffered, he speaks softly:

"Never accepting me for who I am...." His father's critical, caustic words force the first rock to fall.

"Zero affection...." No hand on the shoulder, no hugs, no pats on the back earn a fist-sized rock flung into the bag.

"No play time...." No playful wrestling, no playing catch, no playing anything—they all warrant another weighty rock. The more Rick remembers, the more he elaborates on what he has missed.

"No father-and-son times...." No hanging out together, no talks about manhood, no career conversations. This drives another rock downward. Rick continues pushing the emotional "replay button" buried in his memory.

"Screaming...." A sudden, fearful flashback causes Rick to wince. All the yelling and verbal attacks generate a sizeable jagged rock.

"Hurting my mother...." His father's grating emotional and verbal abuse sends a sizeable sandstone dropping into the bag.

"Get out of my sight!..." His devaluing, denigrating words propel a big hefty boulder.

"Rejection...." sums up the emotional impact of all his father's wounding. Momentum drives a very large, hard rock into Rick's bag. It crashes against the other rocks inside, leaving some small, sharp-edged fragments. Jagged pieces are painfully wedged in Rick's memory. Ultimately, *rejection says it all.*

Expanding on the visual, I tell Rick he has a bag of rocks residing in his soul. For years he has been hauling rocks of resentment, stones of hostility, and boulders of bitterness. Then I point to the bag hanging from the hook around his neck—the burlap now straining from the weight of the rocks.

"What would happen if you were to keep walking around with that bag of rocks hanging onto your hook the rest of your life?"

He immediately responds, needing no time to think, "I wouldn't be able to run anymore." I am surprised and glad at his answer. Instead of saying, "I would become bent over," or "It would be difficult to walk," Rick, the devoted athlete, expresses concern that he could no longer run.

His response articulates so well the cost of failing to get rid of cumbersome "rocks." Think of all the scriptures that refer to running. The apostle Paul says, "Do you not know that in a race all the runners run, but only one gets the prize? Run in such a way as to get the prize."[2] And he asked, "You were running a good race.

> When we forgive, we get rid of the rocks dragging us down and depleting our strength.

Who cut in on you and kept you from obeying the truth?"[3]

What Rick said from a physical standpoint—"I wouldn't be able to run anymore"—is just as true emotionally and spiritually. Weighed down by too many rocks, the best we would be able to do is trudge our way through life. If more rocks are added to the pile, we'll barely be able to move forward. And if even more rocks are thrown on the heap, we will completely collapse under the weight.

But when we learn to forgive—even when we don't feel like it—we get rid of the rocks dragging us down and depleting our strength. As we work through the process of forgiveness, we are set free from the pressure of the strain...we feel unshackled...we feel released...we feel free!

The prophet Isaiah describes what this freedom is like: "They will soar on wings like eagles; *they will run* and not grow weary, they will walk and not faint."[4]

Now back to Rick: The last thing I want to do is leave this wounded young man weighed down by emotional pain. I want to see him run!

"Rick, do you want to live the rest of your life carrying all this pain from your past?"

"No, I don't."

"Then are you willing to take all the past pain off of your hook and place it onto God's hook?"

"Yes, I am."

"Would you be willing to take your father off of your emotional hook and place him onto God's hook?"

"Yes, I want to."

In prayer, we both go before God's throne of grace. "Lord Jesus," I start.

"Lord Jesus," he echoes, "thank You for caring about my heart… and how much I've been hurt…You know the pain I have felt… because of my father's treatment…his anger…his lack of affection… his abuse…his rejection."

All of a sudden, throughout the crowd, the unexpected occurs. As Rick repeats the prayer, making it his own, an undercurrent of prayers—barely above a whisper—waft across the room. Goose bumps rise on my arms. Feeling a holy sense of awe, I realize that on this day, more than one bag of rocks is soon to be empty.

"Lord, I release all this pain into Your hands….Thank You, Lord Jesus…for dying on the cross for me…and extending Your forgiveness to me…. As an act of my will…I choose to forgive my father."

As Rick continues to pray, a remarkable change takes place. His voice, initially reserved, swells with determined strength.

"I choose to take my father…off of my emotional hook…and right now, I place him…onto Your hook…. I refuse all thoughts of revenge…. I trust that in Your time You will deal with my father… just as You see fit. And thank You, Lord, for giving me…Your power to forgive…so that I can be set free…. In Your holy name I pray. Amen."

Rick's tears of gratitude reveal he is now experiencing the freedom of forgiveness. And at this same time, through the power of forgiveness, many bags of bitterness throughout the auditorium have been emptied.

Personally, I know what it feels like to be weighed down with the rocks of resentment. If you, too, feel such a weight, I understand. Just know, the words within this book are written with one goal in mind—*to leave you with an empty bag.*

2

THE SCHOOL
OF HARD ROCKS

Stockpiling My Stones of Spite

THE DECISION TO WRITE about the pain of my childhood was not made quickly or easily. I have written on many other topics without divulging details about my growing-up years. However, as a matter of integrity, I cannot write a book on forgiveness without explaining this painful period—without sharing memories that for years stuck like shards in my soul, deadening my emotions.

The most overwhelming tests in my life have involved my relationship with my father, a man who was hard as flint and whose anger could spark at even the slightest annoyance. Without these *tests*, I would have no *test*imony—especially regarding forgiveness. And without a testimony, there would be no platform for the ministry God has given me. Mine is a story of learning to forgive…even when I didn't feel like it.

I grew up in a family full of secrets—secrets we dared not discuss with one another, much less friends. Our family was dysfunctional, full of fear and facades, dissension and disruption. My father's frequent and flagrant acts of immorality went totally unchecked. Throughout my tumultuous growing-up years, Mother held the most precious place in my heart. She was unfailingly kind, gracious, and loving. I adored her.

My father, on the other hand, was an enormous success in his professional life, but an enormous failure in his family life. He had a looming, larger-than-life presence, always seen in his business "uniform"—navy blue suit, light blue shirt, blue bow tie—which he wore every day, seven days a week. He was recognized as a visionary leader who provided hundreds of jobs through his various business ventures.

While considered a great man by many outside our home, he was viewed as an oppressive man inside our home. So unpredictable was his temper that around him, we were all eggshell-walkers.

Rocks of resentment accumulated in my bag on a regular basis.

When my father became romantically involved with my mother, he was more than twice her age. Unbeknownst to her, he was a married man with six children, the second-born being her age. My mother's father had died of tuberculosis when she was just three years old; therefore, I believe she lived with a father-void in her

Reshaping a Hardened Heart

Flint is a hard, sedimentary form of quartz with a glassy appearance, and its color can vary—dark brown, gray, blue, or black. When struck against metal, its sparks ignite gunpowder. When hit with another hard object, its "splinters" or "blades" can be shaped into sharp arrowheads and knives. For centuries, flint has also been used to build stone walls.

Unforgiveness can make your heart hard and dark like flint, and over time, you can amass enough bitterness to build an impenetrable wall around your soul. But when you surrender your hardened heart to the Master Stonecutter, He reshapes your heart *to look like His*—sensitive to the needs of others.

Only by dislodging the flint from your fortified wall and giving it to the Lord will He refigure your heart to be like His. Realize that rather than condemnation, He offers compassion. Rather than judgment, He extends mercy. By releasing the flint into His hands—the flint of unforgiveness—He will reshape your hardened heart and *make it like His*.

heart. This void made her vulnerable to a persistent, persuasive father-figure—even after she became aware that the relationship was wrong.

We lived as his covert family on the side—Mother and we four children, me being the second-born. Over time, our secret became a big rock to bear, eroding my sense of security.

For the first 12 years of my life, I grew up with a different last name—I was June Wright. Dad said we were "the Wright family" because he and Mother were doing what was *right*. However, for years Mother lived with both unrelenting guilt and horrendous shame.

Every Sunday, she drove us to church, and although she deeply longed to go inside, she felt much too unworthy. She would walk us children to the door, but then she would stay outside. Shame poured from every pore of her being. Many times I saw agony on her face. Her tender heart was no match for my father's power, abuse, and fear tactics. She felt trapped with no way out.

All during those early years, I ached for my mother—she had no friend, no confidant. Although I was not a Christian at the time, I remember praying, "God, please give my mother a friend." She felt afraid to have friends because she was fearful of bringing shame upon them.

One December, a year after Dad's first wife died, he brought us all to live in his house. The following November, Dad married Mother and soon afterward, I became known as June Hunt.

You would think this change in circumstance would have made things simpler, but it didn't. Sometimes I got stuck not knowing how to answer sensitive family questions such as, "Is he your real father or not?" My "new name" was difficult to explain because my birth certificate already read Ruth June Hunt. No one coached me.

Subsequently, my bag of rocks only grew increasingly heavy.

Dad was excessively possessive of Mother. Beautiful, submissive, and charming, she was the classic "trophy wife." He proudly showed her off to his frequent dinner guests. She shone like a jewel against the dark backdrop of my father's granite disposition.

We four were forbidden to speak at mealtimes—"Children are to be seen, not heard"—unless there was a topic of conversation that would be of interest to everyone. Since nothing we said was ever of interest to Dad, we rarely spoke. Many stones of aggravation fell into my bag, especially during dinner. What's more, Dad told me numerous times, "You are a bad influence on your mother." Or sometimes he would say, "All of you children are a bad influence on your mother!" So immediately after dinner we had to go upstairs, stay in our rooms, and study. We were not allowed to see Mother.

This nightly restriction created sizeable stones to bear—especially for my younger sisters, Helen and Swanee.

Mother's heart ached over Dad's possessiveness and all his prohibitions. After dinner, she would use any excuse to run upstairs in order to make the rounds, room by room...checking on us, hugging us, encouraging us. Nurturing our tender hearts was her true priority—although Dad denied her that right.

In contrast, the compassion required to nurture a child was not found in Dad.

Our family had a little silver poodle named Bambi. I loved her dearly. She was my best friend—the only one with whom I had ever shared my heart. As a freshman in high school, I needed to write an English paper. For the first time ever, I decided to get inspiration at a nearby lake.

Paper finished and walking back, I saw something unidentifiable in the road. As I got closer, all I could exclaim was, "No...no...no!" I had no idea that Bambi had followed me. To my horror, my little confidant had been hit by a car and killed.

My heart was crushed. Sobbing with grief, I picked up her limp body and slowly walked back home in a daze. As I approached the door, Dad walked up from the opposite direction, having just arrived from work. He saw me sobbing with lifeless Bambi in my arms.

Rather than offering words of comfort, he tore into me. "How could you be so stupid? Bambi is dead because of you! Look what you did!"

His scathing rebuke spewed forth like lava scorching my already broken heart. Bam!

To make matters worse, hurtful words gushed out again, "Crying is a sign of mental illness—stop crying!" At that moment, in my traumatized state, I knew I must not cry one more tear—so I didn't. And for years, I would not allow myself to cry, even though I knew such suppression was unhealthy.

Dad's repeated volcanic eruptions culminated in layer upon layer of solidified molten rock in my emotional bag.

It's hard to admit, but I hated my father with a seething rage. At age 15, I posed a veiled question to a friend's father who was a lawyer. "If a 15-year-old boy commits murder, what would happen to him?"

"Well, at 15, he's a minor, so he would probably be sent to juvenile detention until he's 18, and then released." That's all I needed to know.

Two weeks later, I approached Mother with a proposition. "Mom, I need to talk with you. I've figured out a way to kill Dad. There won't be much repercussion on me because I'm a minor." I was dead serious.

I'm so grateful for my mother's response. She did not chide me, laugh at me, or ridicule me. Instead, she sympathetically said, "No, honey, I appreciate what you're trying to do, but that really won't be necessary." It's not that I wanted to commit murder—I just wanted the pain to stop.

Perhaps getting rid of Dad would help me get rid of all my rocks, stones, and boulders.

In truth, my mother and I experienced a role reversal as I tried to be her protector. But no matter how hard I tried, I didn't have the power to keep her safe. Sometimes Dad would come into my bedroom and dogmatically allege, "Your mother is mentally ill today." Cringing at his words, I knew to take his words seriously— his eldest son from his first marriage had been institutionalized for years with paranoid schizophrenia.

Rocks of rancor fell into my bag every time he made such frightening statements.

I knew on one particular day, Mother had tears in her eyes because Dad was flaunting one of his "women friends" named Ginger. I knew tears were not a sign of mental illness. However, my concern was this. Dad had money, money buys power, power buys people. I was deathly afraid Dad would buy off a psychiatrist to institutionalize Mother.

Dad terrorized Mother, not just by asserting she was mentally ill, but also by taking her to different psychiatrists. Although no doctor ever diagnosed Mother with any kind of mental disorder, just the mention of mental illness struck terror in her heart—and mine. For years, these boulders weighed me down.

> When I came home from school each day, I never knew if Mother would be there.

When I came home from school each day, I never knew if Mother would be there. I feared Dad really would have her institutionalized one day. Early on, I began my defense fund. I knew if he ever had her committed, I'd need to hire a lawyer to get her out. For years I would never buy a Coke or candy bar. Instead, every penny I possessed went into "The Defense Fund."

I lived in daily dread of what might happen to Mom. Until one day, in the midst of one of Dad's rampages about Mother's mental state, I lost it. "Has it ever occurred to you that *you* might be the one mentally ill?" I sniped.

Instantly, my father retaliated physically. I was stunned. His actions devastated me. Yet I was determined he would not make me cry, and he didn't. I won!...until the next morning, and then *bam*—the biggest boulder of all fell into my already-bulging bag. My father sent me away to boarding school for several months. I was only ten minutes away from home, but I might as well have been in Siberia.

Dad often spat out accusations toward or about all of us. Several summers in a row he matter-of-factly stated to me, "You and your sisters are bad influences on your mother. I'm sending you away to camp."

To *get to go* to camp is one matter—being *sent away* to camp is another. Because this camp was in Colorado, every mention of Colorado evoked a sickening feeling within me. While at camp, I never knew if Mother would be permanently gone when I returned home.

The "bad influence" accusations, the threats to have Mom institutionalized, the isolation of boarding school, being exiled to summer camp—the stones of disdain continued to pile up, one on top of another.

I know what it's like to literally think, *I may be going crazy.* As a newly licensed teenager, I remember driving our car across a bridge, thinking, *I could just turn the wheel and go over the side. I could end my life right now.* But then I feared I could cripple myself, and that would be worse on Mom.

Dad's perpetual pummeling was driving me to the edge.

Finding God in the Darkness

Over time, I began hearing people in several places talk about the difference between having a *religion* versus a *relationship* with God. I had no idea what they meant. Although I had attended church, I never had heard about true salvation, never read the Bible, never learned about authentic Christianity.

For six months, I closely observed a number of these people who clearly had "something" I didn't have but wanted. As a result, I began to seriously examine the claims of Christ. For months I grappled with question after question and wrestled with issue after issue until I finally decided to entrust my life to Jesus and give Him control of my life.

To my surprise, Christ *inside me* started *changing me*—inside out. My distorted view of life began to be corrected. My entire perspective started to change as I understood who Jesus was and what He said.

Changing My Attitude Toward Dad

But there was one issue that plagued me. Because I loved math and equations, I had this formula all worked out: God hates sin. Dad is sinning. God hates Dad. I hate Dad. My formula was all so very logical—I naturally should hate Dad because God hates Dad.

Being a new Christian, I began devouring truth from God's Word. I began to learn a lot about love: We are to love one another and even love our enemies. However, I truly believed my situation was the exception, that my negative feelings toward Dad were legitimate, and that God "understood." I didn't feel like forgiving, so I didn't.

> We are to love one another and even love our enemies.

Then I was stopped dead in my tracks by this scripture: "Anyone who claims to be in the light but hates his brother is still in the darkness.... whoever hates his brother is in the darkness and walks around in the darkness; he does not know where he is going, because the darkness has blinded him."[1]

Obviously, that verse explicitly refers to hatred. I thought, *Well, that's true...but God knows my situation. He knows I can't help but hate Dad!*

But there was only one problem—God has a standard: Hate no one. God does not set aside His holy standard based on anyone's situation. There are no "situation ethics" regarding the Bible—it's either true or it's not. I came to realize that God wasn't going to make an exception for me just because of a father with a heart of stone.

By this point, my mother was growing dramatically in her Christian faith because of her intimate relationship with Jesus, meaningful Bible study, and strong Christian friends who had come into her life and loved her unconditionally.

One day, when feeling perturbed at Dad, I went to Mom and asked, "How can you be so nice to him?" Never will I forget her response—spoken with the utmost tenderness and compassion. "Oh, honey, he doesn't have the Lord. If he just had the Lord, he wouldn't be that way."

I was stunned. How could my mother, who had been mercilessly mistreated, be so genuinely loving? The answer was simple: *She looked beyond his fault and saw his need.* And clearly, he needed the Lord in his life. Her Christlike perspective enabled me to begin looking beyond his fault to see his need for the Savior.

Getting Rid of the Rocks

Though I will never have all my questions answered as to what motivated my father's abusive behavior, years after his death I discovered a telling truth: Dad himself was raised in a home filled with emotional and physical abuse.

And because his own father was physically violent, he had no modeling of how to be a caring, nurturing father. This discovery provided great insight. His home had been built on shifting sand rather than solid rock—the rock of biblical truth.

Through my growing-up years, I carried an emotionally heavy bag filled with stones of scorn, rocks of wrath, and boulders of bitterness. However, God's power enabled me to do what I thought I could not do: truly and completely forgive my father.

Unforgiveness weighed me down and kept me in bondage, whereas forgiveness emptied my load and set me free. *Getting rid of the rocks*—the rocks of resentment—liberated me to experience lightness within my soul and true peace with God.

3

"Stone Her! Stone Her!"

*What Forgiveness Is,
What Forgiveness Isn't*

THE DUST RISES IN A THICK CLOUD around the angry crowd stomping through the streets. Emotions are heated, tempers flare to a fever pitch.

Shouts of "Stone her! Stone her!" echo off the rock streets and stone walls. At the front of the mob, a frightened, frantic woman trembles. Her faint cries for mercy are drowned out by the demanding voices around her insisting on justice.

But justice isn't all this crowd wants. They plan to use this woman to set a trap for the troublemaker, the Jewish teacher known as Jesus. His radical message of forgiveness and mercy is about to be put to the test.

The mob finally reaches the place at the temple where Jesus is teaching. The woman's captors thrust her before Him. The accusers encircle them both like a pack of snarling wolves.

These scribes and Pharisees publicly announce the charge against her: "Adultery—caught in the very act!" Only one outcome is possible: death by stoning. The law literally requires it.

"What do *you* say?" demand the religious rulers, daring Jesus to refute the law and thereby condemn Himself.

The Teacher says nothing. He stays seated. Then, bending over, He writes in the dirt with His finger.

These self-righteous rulers—confident that the law is on their side—press Him again. "She was caught in adultery, in the very act! *What do you say?*"

Finally, Jesus speaks with a calm knowing: "Let him who is without sin among you be the first to throw a stone at her."

Bending down again, He continues writing in the dirt.

No one moves. Moments pass. The very ones so eager to stone the woman slither away one by one until she is left alone with Jesus.

Now He stands up and asks with no hint of judgment, "Where are your accusers? Did no one condemn you?"

"No one, Lord," she answers.

"Neither do I condemn you." His voice is filled with compassion. "Go and sin no more."[1]

This adulterous woman, who moments before knew she was destined to die, now finds herself totally free—free *only* because of forgiveness.

Facing certain death from the rock throwers, she received refuge—her life was saved by Jesus, the Redeemer, the Rock of Refuge. She could well have said, "The LORD is my rock, my fortress and my deliverer; my God is my rock, in whom I take refuge. He is my shield and the horn of my salvation, my stronghold."[2]

≈

This timeless, life-changing account of how Jesus forgave the adulterous woman beautifully illustrates the heart of God toward people and His eagerness to cancel our debt of sin.

Eagerness? Yes. Jesus did not reluctantly or begrudgingly forgive her—He did not *prefer* to punish her. He *desired* to grant this known sinner—caught in the act—total grace and mercy. He desired that she, in turn, would take to heart His words to "go and sin no more" so she would no longer live the life of a "scarlet woman."

This passage of Scripture is filled with the heart of compassion and the hope of forgiveness. Our own hearts are moved that this condemned woman need not die because of her sins. We are affected by her story of forgiveness because it reveals that we, too, can be forgiven.

In truth, no one wants to be like the stone throwers in this story. However, we are like them when we won't loosen our grip—when we won't let our stones fall to the ground. As a result of not releasing our stones, *we continue to bear a burdensome weight.*

> By clearing away the confusion about forgiveness, we lay the foundation for our own freedom.

We want others to drop their stones, but we are reluctant to drop our stones. This reluctance is often based on misconceptions about what forgiveness is and isn't.

What Forgiveness Is Not

By clearing away some of the confusion about forgiveness, we lay the foundation for our own freedom—the stone wall encasing our hearts can be broken, freeing us from our rocks of resentment and enabling us to love and be loved.

Let's explore seven misunderstandings about forgiveness.[3]

1. *Forgiveness is not a natural response— but rather supernatural*

Countless times, people have told me, "I *can't* forgive. I just can't." And I reply, "You could be right—*you* can't. But Christ in you *can.*"

So many people try to do it alone when it comes to forgiveness. They try to muster their own strength and determination…but still seethe with resentment and rage. Why? Because they haven't allowed Christ to give them *His strength* to forgive. They don't know that when they totally entrust their lives to Christ, they can claim, "I can do everything *through Him* who gives me *strength.*"[4]

No wonder they feel inadequate. The most common mistake we make is failing to recognize that in order to forgive as God forgives, we need both His presence and His power. If there's one thing that isn't natural for us, it's forgiveness. We need to surrender to God's will and tap into His strength. *Only then can we drop our stones, never to pick them up again.*

2. *Forgiveness is not the same as reconciliation*

Some people sincerely but mistakenly assume that if they forgive an offender, they *must* re-establish the relationship. Unfortunately, this mistaken mind-set has kept countless victims from forgiving their victimizers.

When God asks us to forgive, He does not mean there must be instant reconciliation. Forgiveness does not mean turning back the clock and starting over as if nothing happened. "Let's just bury the hatchet and go back to the way things were."

Of course, forgiveness *can* lead to reconciliation, and quite often does. But sometimes reconciliation is not warranted or even possible, especially in cases involving severe abuse, sexual immorality, or if the offender refuses to change.

Forgiveness is one-way, and reconciliation is two-way. Reconciliation is a process that succeeds only when both parties are willing to work at it. Forgiveness, on the other hand, is a personal decision on the part of the victim regardless of the offender's decisions.

Reconciliation requires a change in the offender's behavior. Forgiveness requires nothing at all from the offender. We can choose to forgive even if it is never sought or deserved.

Forgiveness depends solely on our willingness to do as the Lord did for us—we unilaterally and unconditionally cancel the debt. We don't bury the hatchet, but we do drop the stones.

3. *Forgiveness is not a feeling*

When Roger called our radio program one night, he said his life was "hanging by a thread." His voice reeked with bitterness and despair. He struggled with tears as he told his story.

Roger had been a successful businessman most of his life. He started in the sales department of a large corporation. Within a few years, he was promoted to manager, overseeing dozens of salesmen on three continents.

After a meteoric rise within the company, Roger decided to risk his prestigious position, large salary, and comfortable benefits to start his own business. He formed a partnership with Blake, one of his most trusted friends, whom he'd known since college. In fact, Blake introduced Roger to Susan, the woman Roger eventually married. Blake was the best man at Roger's wedding.

The new business was incredibly successful, exceeding everyone's expectations. It tripled in size and earnings in two years and was set to keep expanding.

Roger felt secure for the first time in his life. He knew he could comfortably pay for his kids to go to college. He and Susan began building a cabin in the majestic mountains of Colorado, a comfortable retreat that would be their retirement home.

Then his world collapsed. Roger received a phone call late one night from his accountant. "I hate to tell you this, but the company is about to go under." Money was missing...*major money.*

Blake had been systematically embezzling significant assets from the business, right under Roger's nose. His partner and "friend" had drained the company dry. Everything Roger had worked so hard to achieve was gone. After months of endless efforts to keep the business solvent, he was forced to declare bankruptcy.

That devastating week, Roger called out of desperation.

"Right now, I can't feel anything but anger and hatred toward Blake. Truthfully, I feel like a volcano ready to erupt. The whole thing's got me tied up in knots. There's no way I could ever feel like forgiving him."

After acknowledging how painful the betrayal must have been, I explained to Roger that *forgiveness is not a feeling.* It is *a decision, an act of the will.* Feelings are not necessary in order to forgive someone's debt against us. We must simply know that God asks us to let go of our claim against an offender—"He has to pay!"—and choose to hand the claim over to Christ.

We need to loosen the grip on our stones and give them to Christ. Is that as easy as it sounds? Absolutely not! Sometimes it's difficult, sometimes it's agonizing. Still we need to forgive—not because it is easy or feels right, but because it is Christ's nature to forgive.

Realize that if you have "Christ in you,"[5] then you have His supernatural nature and power at your disposal to enable you to do what you feel you cannot do! That is why the apostle Peter says, "His divine power has given to us all things that pertain to life and godliness." And this is only possible because we are "partakers of the

---

Releasing Your Grip

Topaz is the hardest silicate mineral and one of the hardest minerals in nature. It is valued for its high luster, variety of color, and multifaceted crystals. Its color spectrum includes yellow, pink, orange, red, brown, blue, and green. But the most stunning and rare is the reddish-orange "Imperial Topaz." In nineteenth-century Russia, only the czar's family was permitted to own this regal rock.

Imagine your fingers tightly squeezing a stone, symbolizing a rock of offense that has left you emotionally immobile. Your grip is so tight you cannot pry even one finger off that stone—and it's because you don't *feel like forgiving*.

But the truth is you can *choose* to forgive as an *act* of your will. You can choose to release your grip and watch God fashion your feelings into a forgiving spirit. You can *choose* to hand that stone over to the Master Miner. From it, He will create something noble, something admirable, something ever more valuable than you could envision—even more valuable than the Imperial Topaz.

divine nature" of Christ Himself.[6] Because it was natural for Christ to forgive, as partakers of His divine nature, we too can forgive.

We too can be stone droppers rather than stone throwers.

4. Forgiveness is not excusing the wrong or letting the guilty "get away with it"

All wrong behavior is wrong! All wrong behavior is without excuse. Too many people have the mistaken mind-set that if they forgive, they will be saying that the offense against them was never wrong.

No! Forgiveness never implies, "What you did is okay—no big deal." When someone wounds us, not only is the offense real, but the emotional pain we incur is also real.

5. Forgiveness is not letting the guilty off the hook

I've heard these words over and over again: "If I forgive, I'm just letting him off the hook!" No. That's not what forgiveness is. It is *moving the guilty from your hook to God's hook.*

We don't have the ability to let the offender off the hook of the potential consequences he or she may face, such as ruined relationships, crippling guilt, social isolation, financial repayment, or even criminal punishment.

> Forgiveness is moving the guilty from your hook to God's hook.

But we can take the person off of *our* emotional hook and put him or her onto God's hook, and trust Him to deal with that person justly and rightly.

We take the person—and the burlap bag containing the rocks of their offenses against us—and give them *all* to God. When we put the burden onto Him, our load is lifted and we are emotionally free. With our hands emptied of stones, they are open to receive the good things God desires to give us.

6. Forgiveness is not being a "doormat" or a weak martyr

Spineless passivity was not the path Jesus took. Feeble acquiescence is not walking in the footsteps of Jesus.

Forgiveness is not being a doormat. If that were so, Jesus would be the greatest doormat of all! Forgiveness is not being a weak martyr. It *is* being strong enough to be Christlike—a sign of godly courage.

Forgiveness is not being wimpy and weak-willed. Jesus was known for His extraordinary forgiveness, and no one—not even one critic of Christ—has ever considered Him a weak-willed wimp.

The weak lash out in mindless revenge, lacking godly wisdom, lacking supernatural restraint. Anyone can attack; anyone can throw stones. But we are called to rely on Christ's presence and power, living within us, to turn the other cheek. By forgiving, we align ourselves with the most powerful being in the universe, God Almighty—for it is He Himself who offers us full forgiveness.

7. Forgiveness has nothing to do with "fairness"

Most people learn by preschool or kindergarten the concept of playing fair. And most of the time—with notable exceptions—our individual lives and social interaction are governed by a code of fairness. Our sporting events are overseen by referees who ensure fair play. We write laws and regulations meant to "level the playing field" so everyone in our society gets an equal shot at success.

Yet when it comes to forgiveness, the word *fairness* can be a huge obstacle. The thinking goes like this: Because the injury I received wasn't fair, it's only reasonable to expect my offender to pay. That person owes me. It would be *unfair* if my offender doesn't suffer as I did.

That, of course, is the world's way, and it seems completely understandable. We like the scales to balance. We like the numbers to add up exactly. We like equality in all things. We want an "eye for an eye" justice.

But that is not God's way. Fairness isn't the issue. After all, it was not "fair" for the heavenly Father to give up His Son on the cross...but He did. It was not "fair" for the Son to give up His life... but He did. Forgiveness has nothing to do with fairness—or else it would not be forgiveness at all! Forgiveness is the *unconditional* dismissal of a debt.

Forgiveness is *dropping* stones when the world says to *throw* them.

What Is Forgiveness?

Imagine you want to go to college. The only problem is you have no money or means to earn enough to reach your goal—graduation. A businessman in your town hears about your dilemma and offers to loan you the money, with the clear understanding that you will pay it back once your education is complete.

The contract you sign states that if you leave school for any reason, the debt is payable immediately. If you cannot pay by a specified date, the matter will be decided by a judge. You gratefully accept and put your signature on the legally binding contract.

You move to a different city to start your life as a student. At first, everything goes according to plan. Your world blossoms with ideas and friendships and exciting possibilities. Little by little, all those possibilities turn into distractions. You stay up too late, then skip a class. Soon, you skip whole days of school and spend more time socializing than studying.

This goes on for weeks. By the end of the first semester, the money you borrowed is gone. How will you continue? How will you eat and pay rent? Your account is empty. Then you're gripped by the most daunting question of all: How will you ever pay the debt you owe?

For a while, you ignore the problem. You sleep on a friend's couch. You take a job washing dishes in the cafeteria, which pays for food but little else. Meanwhile, your lender catches wind that something is wrong. He calls, then writes, asking for an update. But you avoid the calls and fail to answer the letters. You reason, *If I give it a little time, things will work out.*

Weeks stretch into months. Suddenly you get another letter—this one from a lawyer. The formal, threatening language informs you that the lender has decided to exercise his right to take you to court to recoup his money. You try every possible way you can think of to raise the money. Nothing works. Out of desperation, you finally write a letter in which you ask for more time. The lawyer replies that the contract is binding. The debt must be paid.

On the day of your court appearance, you have lost all hope. You know you were wrong to burn through the money, and you have no way of making things right. You are prepared to accept whatever the judge says. You take a seat in the courtroom, noticing immediately that your lender and his lawyer are not present.

The judge enters and asks you to approach the bench. Your stomach churns, your legs wobble, but you comply. This is it—time to suffer the consequences. The judge begins to smile and says, "Your debt has been forgiven. The case is dismissed." He then mentions that a brief letter was sent from your lender along with the original contract.

> Your debt is forgiven. You are free of your obligation. Do with this contract what you want.

Stunned, you walk away. It slowly sinks in that you have been set free. There's nothing hanging over your head, no burdensome weight dragging you down. You can start over. Joy overtakes you as you walk out of the courtroom into the bright daylight. Suddenly, you stop and resolve to do whatever it takes to reclaim your life, redouble your efforts, and regain the faith once placed in you.

Forgiveness Is the Dismissal of Debt

The New Testament Greek word for forgiveness, *aphesis*, means a "pardon, cancellation of an obligation, punishment or guilt." Forgiveness is one person canceling the debt of another person. In life, an unforgiven offense is an unpaid debt—a psychological, emotional, and even spiritual debt between two people. Therefore, unforgiveness is a link that *binds the two together. Neither are free from it.*

When we forgive, we not only dismiss the debt we are owed, but we also trust God to

> Learning to forgive someone is nothing short of learning to think and act like God.

handle the offender in His time and in His way as He sees fit. He assures us, "It is mine to avenge; I will repay."[7]

God forgives our debt of sin and rebellion against Him. The apostle Paul says, "Blessed are they whose transgressions are *forgiven*, whose sins are covered. Blessed is the man whose sin the Lord will never count against him."[8] No doubt we were guilty as charged and in no way could we ever pay the penalty on our own.

God had every right to hold us to the letter of the law and demand that we pay with our lives. Instead, Jesus cancelled the debt by paying it Himself, shedding His own blood in place of ours. In doing so, He set us totally free from the consequences of falling short of His standards.

Jesus took our place. His body was pelted by the stones of our offenses, the stones that should have been thrown at us. All the stones others have collected to throw at us and we have collected to throw at them have already been thrown at Jesus. That is why He rightfully asks us all to not throw stones at one another but to give the stones to Him.

David, who knew the desperate need to be forgiven, wrote,

> He does not treat us as our sins deserve or repay us according to our iniquities. For as high as the heavens are above the earth, so great is his love for those who fear him; as far as the east is from the west, so far has he removed our transgressions from us.[9]

It is impossible to imagine any forgiveness more complete than that.

Learning to forgive someone who has wronged us is nothing short of learning *to think and act like God.*

Unforgiveness hardens our hearts and weighs us down. When we repeatedly refuse to forgive, more and more offenses accumulate, which become like layers of hardened cement. As we forgive, one offense at a time, the cement cracks and falls away, and more and more, our hearts begin to resemble the heart of God.

Jesus said, "Come to Me, all you who labor and are *heavy laden,* and I will give you rest."[10] Unforgiveness becomes a heavy load for us; it's like lugging around a gargantuan bag of cement. Neither party can be free of the burden as long as the debt remains on the books.

Forgiveness Is Releasing Your Resentment and Rights

Imagine that you are a runner in the Olympics. You have the right shoes, right shorts, right shirt. Yet something is desperately wrong. Locked on your ankle is a heavy black ball and chain! You can't run the distance, you can't even qualify. If only you could free yourself...but you don't have the key to unlock the chain.

Then on the day of the qualifying run, you are told that you already possess the key to freedom. Quickly, you free yourself, and, oh, what freedom! It is as though that black ball miraculously turns into a big helium balloon. The load is lifted, the balloon is released, the weight is sent away.

Previously, no one had told you that your unforgiveness was the black ball weighing you down. Now that you know forgiveness is one of the major keys to freedom, you can run the race...and cross the finish line with freedom. "Let us throw off everything that hinders and the sin that so easily entangles, and let us run with perseverance the race marked out for us."[11]

To forgive means to *release your resentment* toward your offender.

In the New Testament, the Greek verb *aphiemi* primarily means "to send away"—in other words, "to *forgive*, send away or release the penalty when someone wrongs you."[12] This implies that you need to release your right to hear "I'm sorry," to release your right to be bitter, to release your right to get even. The Bible says, "Do not repay anyone evil for evil. Be careful to do what is right in the eyes of everybody."[13]

To forgive is to *release your rights* regarding the offense. This means to release your right to dwell on the offense, to release your right to hold on to the offense, to release your right to keep bringing up the offense. The book of Proverbs says it well: "He who covers over an offense promotes love, but whoever repeats the matter separates close friends."[14]

A True Story of the Power of Forgiveness

"Thomas" and his wife "Catherine" had become grim fixtures in their pastor's office. Only a few months had passed since Catherine admitted to having an affair. The pain cut Thomas to the core. Although Catherine felt deep anguish over her sin, she continued to struggle with romantic feelings for her lover, and remained confused over her conflicting emotions. Thomas had a decision to make. He knew he had biblical grounds for divorce, but the welfare of the couple's six- and eight-year-old daughters weighed heavily on his heart.

Though Catherine vowed the affair was over, Thomas canceled her cell phone service and cut off her home Internet access. But he knew that these safeguards were only superficial. For their marriage to survive, hard work would be required on both of their parts—gut-wrenching work. Catherine would need to demonstrate true repentance, with no future contact, and Thomas would need to somehow forgive her. But was that really possible? His feelings of anger, grief, and betrayal were overwhelming. And what about being able to trust her again? He wanted to, and knew he needed to. But how could he while carrying such deep wounds in his heart?

The couple's pastor suggested Thomas and Catherine attend our Biblical Counseling Institute, where that month's topic just so happened to be forgiveness. Thomas agreed to attend but Catherine declined, saying the girls needed her—they'd become insecure and vulnerable in the wake of the couple's obvious emotional turmoil. Thomas decided to go alone.

Giant boulders of anger and betrayal pounded upon Thomas's heart—colliding with his desire for peace and freedom. But as he listened that night, Thomas learned that forgiveness didn't mean letting Catherine off the hook. Rather, it meant taking her off *his* emotional hook and placing her on *God's* hook.

At the close of the conference, I pointed to a cluster of white helium balloons in the corner and gave each participant a card. "If you are truly willing to forgive, then write the name of your offender on the card and tie the card to the bottom of the string," I told the group. "Then go outside and intentionally release the balloon as a symbol of releasing your offender—and the offenses— to God."

Still holding their balloons as they approached the doorway, Thomas and his pastor talked about how they were impacted by what they had just heard. Once outside, Thomas paused abruptly, peering up into the chilly night sky. A peaceful smile parted his lips as, slowly, he lifted the balloon heavenward. After a few moments, he released it. "There it goes," he whispered, his pastor bearing silent witness. Their eyes gazed upward as Thomas's balloon gently sailed out of sight and, with it, a small white card that simply read, "Catherine."

In the year that followed, God did an amazing thing in their lives. "Catherine felt Thomas's genuine forgiveness and faithfulness, and Catherine has truly repented," the pastor said. "Her relationship with the Lord has really grown and, in turn, Thomas's trust in

Catherine has been almost completely restored...and the children have regained a sense of security."

Thomas and Catherine have "graduated" from the school of hard rocks—not that they don't pick up a pebble or two along the way. But when they do, they know what to do with each one...so that their bags stay light and their spirits free.

"What Father Gives His Child a Stone?"

Extraordinary Love, Extraordinary Forgiveness

Not long ago, researchers from Baylor University released the results of a study that examined the different views people have of God. The study included a survey conducted by the Gallup organization that identified four distinct perceptions of God's nature and character. The findings were as follows:

- Those who believe in an "Authoritarian God" who is "angry at humanity's sins": 31.4 percent.

- Those who believe in a "Distant God" who is more of a "cosmic force that launched the world then left it spinning on its own": 24.4 percent.

- Those who believe in a "Critical God" who "has his judgmental eye on the world": 16 percent.

- Those who believe in a "Benevolent God" who is forgiving and accepting of anyone who repents: 23 percent.[1]

Amazing, isn't it? If we can extrapolate those survey results to the larger population, we conclude that nearly three-fourths of people in our society view God negatively, using words such as angry, distant, and judgmental to describe Him. Less than one-fourth view Him as loving, accepting, and forgiving.

≈

The God we read about in the Bible is a Creator whose very character is rooted in generosity, grace, and goodness. He is a loving Father who *wants* us to come to Him...who *wants* us to ask of Him...who *wants* us to depend on Him. He *delights* in forgiving our sins and meeting our needs.

In the Gospel of Matthew, Jesus compares the goodness of an earthly father to the goodness of our heavenly Father. "Which one of you, if his son asks him for bread, will *give him a stone?*...If you then, who are evil, know how to give good gifts to your children, how much more will your Father who is in heaven give good things to those who ask him!"[2]

And of the many good things we need—what more do we need than forgiveness? And from whom do we need forgiveness more than God?

Let's be honest: God's forgiveness is so far-reaching and all-encompassing that it's incomprehensible...inexplicable...inconceivable.

From our human standpoint, God's forgiveness makes no sense. It can't be bought, sold, bartered, measured, or rationed. There is no scientific formula to determine when and to whom it applies. Like air in the atmosphere, it is freely available to anyone *willing* to breathe it in.

To put it another way, God's forgiveness is *extraordinary*.

What Does God's Forgiveness Look Like?

To rational, logical minds, extraordinary forgiveness is shocking and, to some, even offensive. It goes against all our instincts. Most societies in our world base their system of justice on equity, scorekeeping, tit for tat, law and order. Competition, not forgiveness, pervades our culture. We learn from an early age to get the upper hand anytime we can and to never loosen our grip. As the cliché goes, "Nice guys finish last." And many people live by the saying, "Don't get mad—get even!"

In contrast, we come upon scriptures that reveal a very different way of life:

- "He does not treat us as our sins deserve or repay us according to our iniquities. For as high as the heavens are above the earth, so great is his love for those who fear him; as far as the east is from the west, so far has he removed our transgressions from us."[3]

- "Who is a God like you, who pardons sin and forgives the transgression....You...hurl all our iniquities into the depths of the sea."[4]

- "There is now no condemnation for those who are in Christ Jesus, because through Christ Jesus the law of the Spirit of life set me free from the law of sin and death."[5]

No wonder some people have a tough time accepting the concept of complete forgiveness—it goes against the grain of human thinking and behavior. And even those who do believe in forgiveness often apply all kinds of qualifiers—conditions of their own making.

God, in His mercy, sent Jesus to be the sacrifice for our sins so we might be the recipients of His extraordinary forgiveness. Thankfully, the time Jesus lived on earth served another purpose as well: to provide a living, breathing example of what forgiveness looks like. Everything He did and said was an attempt to explain it and exemplify it.

> Jesus was always willing to forgive—*always*.

Throughout His life, Jesus offered hope to the hopeless. He lifted the downcast, befriended the friendless, loved the unlovely, accepted the rejected, healed the sick, saved the sinner, and even forgave those who crucified Him.

Jesus was always willing to forgive—*always*. We rarely feel like forgiving. We're reluctant to forgive. We struggle. We clasp our fingers tightly around the tiniest pebble of offense—but not Jesus.

Not once did He carry even one rock, much less drag around a rock-strewn bag of resentment and bitterness—a bag that could have had countless names written all over it, including yours and mine.

Every step of the way, Jesus stood up to religious leaders who were determined to keep people in bondage through guilt and shame. Over and over, with words and actions, Jesus said, in essence, "You are *offered* total and complete forgiveness. Nothing will stand between you and God's love. No exceptions. No fine print. No opt-out clauses." There is nothing you can do to change His extraordinary love.

Read through the Gospels, and you will see that Jesus barely went a single day without causing the Pharisees and their brood to choke on His message of extraordinary love and forgiveness.

Once, for example, He was teaching a crowd of people when the Pharisees showed up to scrutinize His words and His ways. "Now the tax collectors and sinners were all drawing near to hear Him. And the Pharisees and the scribes grumbled, saying, 'This man receives sinners and eats with them.' "[6]

"That can't be right!" they practically howled. "Did He just say what I think He said?"

As a matter of fact, He did.

How did Jesus respond to this grousing and griping? He told a story to illuminate His intentions—a story that could have unfolded like this...

A Tale of Love and Forgiveness

A young man seethes with resentment as he dumps another bucket of feed over the fence for his father's livestock. He's sick of doing this dirty work—like a slave in his own home. He deserves better. He knows he could make a better life for himself if only...

But wait. Maybe it *is* possible! He makes up his mind then and there to try. He drops the empty bucket and defiantly goes straight to his father.

"I can't take it anymore. I want to live my life, not yours. You have my brother to carry on here. Give me the inheritance that belongs to me so I can make my own way in the world."

The father considers his son's appeal with sadness. He knows the horizon always looks more inviting than the ground underfoot, and he knows his son is not prepared to tackle the temptations out in the world. There is much the lad needs to know and much the father desires to teach him.

Yet to the young and rebellious, adventure always waits *somewhere else*. And the father understands that once the boy decides to leave home in search of excitement, only the experience—not the words—can teach him anything. So, prizing his son above his possessions, the father grants his son's request.

"You are free to go," he says. The son walks away with the full inheritance he would have received at his father's death.

The young man is thrilled at his long-awaited freedom. He gathers up everything that is his and sets off for a distant country. The road is just as exciting as he thought it would be. He tastes food he'd never had and drinks exotic wines. He meets interesting people—warriors, merchants, storytellers, foreigners who speak strange languages. Not to mention the women.

I was right! he says to himself. *This life is wonderful. I was a fool not to leave my father's house sooner.*

He spends his money freely on every entertainment and pleasure he can find, never noticing his wallet growing lighter each day. Then, after a year or two, famine comes to where he has settled. His life of feasts and frivolity comes to a sudden halt. Food grows so scarce that a loaf of bread costs a week's wages. The young man quickly exhausts all the money he has left just to feed himself. Now he has nowhere to turn.

In desperation, he hires himself out to a local landowner.

It's only temporary, he tells himself on the first day, hungry and cold. *One day I'll own a place of my own and the good life will return.*

His new employer leads him outside to the stables. The young man feels a knot in his stomach as he's handed a rough wooden bucket—just like the one back home. Only now, the landowner points to his field of pigs, then leaves.

For days, the young man tends the pigs in the cold. He is so hungry that he considers stealing slop meant for the animals. Every time he lifts the bucket to pour it into the troughs, he's reminded of the life left behind.

"My father's servants have more than enough to eat while I am starving to death!" Then, just as many months before, he makes up his mind to change his life. "I will go home and confess everything. I'll say to my father, 'I have sinned against you. I am no longer worthy to be called your son. Just treat me as one of your servants and let me come home.'"

He sets off immediately—with only a hint of hope.

Meanwhile, his father is watching the road. He has never given up hope that, one day, his son will return. Sure enough, one day, he sees his son approaching! Love and compassion well up within him. Without hesitation, he runs to embrace his boy.

"I have sinned against you, Father. You should no longer think of me as your son. Just let me live with your servants."

"Nonsense! You are my son! You are forgiven!" He calls for a fine robe to be put on his son's shoulders and a ring on his hand. He orders a huge feast for that very night.

The young man's older brother is working in the fields while all this is taking place. When he returns that evening, he is surprised by the high-spirited music and dancing. He asks a servant, "What's going on?"

"Your brother has returned! Your father has ordered the fattened calf killed and a feast is on!"

The older son is bitterly angry at the news and he refuses to come to the celebration. Upon hearing this, his father seeks him out.

"Father, all these years I have been loyal to you. I have worked hard without complaint, and you never gave me so much as a goat to celebrate with my friends. Now this ingrate comes home, this so-called son of yours who wasted your money on prostitutes, and you throw the biggest party I've ever seen! It isn't fair!"

The wise man gently lays a hand on his son's shoulder. He knows that this is one of those times when the need for mercy is greater than the need for justice—even if his son cannot see it.

"My son, you are always with me, and all that is mine is yours," he says, with tears in his eyes. "It is fitting to celebrate and be glad, for this your brother was dead, and is alive; he was lost, and is found."[7]

It is hard to imagine a more moving picture of God's love than the image of this father ecstatically running to meet his wayward son even before the boy could utter a word of repentance. The servants must think the father has "lost it" when they see him take off, bounding and whooping across the fields. It's no secret the father had been deeply hurt by his son's rebellion. Now it's apparent that he had *long ago forgiven the offense*. Why? Not because it was just or fair or profitable, and not because the boy did anything to earn or deserve it. He forgave because of his deep, unconditional love.

> It is nearly impossible to forgive someone without a proper understanding of God's unconditional love.

Paul surely understood this when he wrote,

> Who shall separate us from the love of Christ?...I am convinced that neither death nor life, neither angels nor demons, neither the present nor the future, nor any powers, neither height nor depth, nor anything else in all creation, will be able to separate us from the love of God that is in Christ Jesus our Lord.[8]

This is the essence of the Christian faith—the extraordinary love of Christ, which is our key to success in regard to forgiveness. It begins here, in our understanding that we are extraordinarily forgiven because we are extraordinarily loved.

Not a Speck of Spite in Sight

Aggregates such as sand, gravel, and crushed stone are commonly used to make concrete and asphalt, and they strengthen whatever substance in which they are mixed. Without aggregates, houses couldn't be soundly constructed and highways couldn't be safely built.

Though tiny particles of sand cannot be seen by the naked eye in a huge batch of concrete, the sand has a purpose for being there.

However, specks of sand serve no purpose if you carry them inside your bag, or your shoe, or your eye. They are obviously misplaced! These specks need to be removed.

We are called to forgive as we have been forgiven—*completely*. Not a speck of spite remaining. When you give your miniscule grudges to God, the Master Builder, He will mix your painful experiences into His master plan to construct the path that is right for you. Realize that even specks of sand can accumulate and make for a heavy load—even specks we don't think are important.

God doesn't want only your rocks and boulders, He wants your specks of sand as well. No matter how little the offense, you are still called to forgive. Every speck of strife needs to go, every particle of spite. Let it go, and give it to God...until there is not a speck of spite in sight.

I believe it is nearly impossible to forgive someone who has deeply hurt us without a proper understanding of God's unconditional forgiveness. As psychologist Everett Worthington writes, "When Jesus set aside his divinity[9] and later gave up his life,[10] he illustrated *nonreciprocal* love at the heart of Christianity. He showed that God initiates salvation for humans out of love."[11]

God's Amazing Grace

We *can* extraordinarily love because we *are* extraordinarily loved.

We *can* extraordinarily forgive because we *are* extraordinarily forgiven. We *can empty every last rock* out of our burlap bags because the Rock Remover designed the bag to be emptied. So, let's look at five key factors we know about forgiveness based on Jesus' example:

1. Forgiveness brings life, not death

The arrival of Jesus on earth ushered in an entirely new era—a new way for people to relate to God. Rather than having a strict code for sacrifices, Christ brought forgiveness and freedom. Rather than living life with a rigid set of rules, Christ brought the gift of grace. His life, death, and resurrection ended the need for the old, harsh era and introduced a new era of liberty and mercy.

The great evangelist D.L. Moody, who lived in the nineteenth century, said this:

> When Moses was in Egypt to punish Pharaoh, he turned the waters into blood. When Christ was on earth he turned the water into wine. That is the difference between law and grace. The law says, "Kill him"; grace says, "Forgive him." Law says, "Condemn him"; Grace says, "Love him."
>
> When the law came out of Horeb three thousand men were destroyed.[12] At Pentecost, under grace, three thousand found life.[13] What a difference! When Moses came to the burning bush, he was commanded to take the shoes from off his feet. When the prodigal came home after sinning, he was given a pair of shoes to put on his feet. I would a thousand times rather be under grace than under the law.[14]

From our vantage point, we can scarcely understand how blessed and fortunate we are to live on *this* side of the B.C./A.D. dividing line. Before Christ, forgiveness was not permanent and the blood sacrifices had to continually be repeated. Then, because of Christ's life, death, and resurrection, He gave to believers in Him forgiveness that is free, complete, and irreversible. How tragic that many are still living as though we are on the B.C. side—as though full forgiveness, permanent forgiveness still cannot be found...as though Christ has still not come.

2. Forgiveness is ongoing and endless

God's forgiveness has no timetable and no expiration date. It is made of ingredients that are timeless: grace and love. As the psalmist wrote, "For the Lord is good and his love endures forever; his faithfulness continues through all generations."[15]

Of all Jesus' disciples, perhaps Simon Peter had the greatest warrior's instinct for justice and vengeance. It was he who rallied to Jesus' defense when the Roman guards came to arrest Him, cutting the ear off the servant of the high priest. And it was he who pressed Jesus one day to explain the limits of forgiveness: "Then Peter came to Him and said, 'Lord, how often shall my brother sin against me, and I forgive him? Up to seven times?' Jesus said to him, 'I do not say to you, up to seven times, but up to seventy times seven.' "[16]

Seventy times seven is not a mathematical equation, but a spiritual one. It is a metaphor that means keep going and don't stop. Many people say, "I'll forgive you this one time, but that's it." But God's willingness to forgive never ends. In other words, we need to cut the bottom out of our burlap bags. Don't let those rocks of resentment pile up. Our Redeemer has removed all the rocks from those who have received Him into their lives. *Now that's extraordinary.*

3. Forgiveness removes the conditions for grace

When Mike came to me after a seminar on forgiveness, five years had gone by since his son's murder. However, for Mike, it might as well have happened yesterday. He was stuck in time, trapped by his inability to forgive those responsible for Richie's death.

"He was a great kid," Mike told me, not attempting to hide the emotion that made his voice shake. "He got good grades in school. He helped neighbors. At church, he was a leader in the youth group.

His friends were all solid Christian kids. That's why when he turned 15, we started letting him go out with them at night. We couldn't hold on to him forever—and we thought it was safe."

One night after a party at church, the kids all piled into a car driven by one of the older boys to go get burgers. Mike reminded Richie of his curfew and then watched him ride away. It was the last time Mike saw him alive.

The police investigation pieced together what happened. After getting something to eat, the driver and two other boys in the car said they had an "errand" to run. It wouldn't take long. They drove downtown to a city park in a rough neighborhood. The boys, including Richie, got out of the car. The errand turned out to be a meeting with a drug dealer. Police concluded it was not the first such meeting because an argument erupted right away between the men in the park and the driver of the car. The dealer pulled out a gun and started shooting. Richie was hit in the chest.

"So many things are wrong about that night," Mike said as his tears flowed. "I try to forgive, but I don't know where to start. I think about the man with the gun and sometimes I know I could forgive him. But then I remember the boys who took Richie there in the first place. What were they thinking? And then I wonder why Richie got out of the car at all. It's all too much. For five years I have been trying to process this, and I can't. I don't know who all to blame or where to draw the line. I might be able to forgive some people involved, but not others."

Struggling with where to draw the line is common when we try to make sense of a horrific situation. We feel we have to draw it somewhere or we'll be overwhelmed.

"I'm sorry, June," Mike said with anger creeping into his voice. "What Jesus asks is just too much. The standard He set is just too high." It was as though a volcano erupted five years ago, and today not a piece of hardened lava had been dislodged from Mike's bag. He still carried the full weight of unforgiveness.

"I think you're right about the standards being too high."

He looked shocked.

"But this turns out to be *good* news. To our irrational minds, the standard Jesus set is so extraordinary that it becomes no standard at all."

I explained that standards are rules we use to judge something. For example, college admissions standards let everyone know what test scores are needed. "If you score high enough, then you can be accepted." The Old Testament law established a flawless standard. No one could live up to it, and all are condemned under it's unreachable demands.

> When we forgive, we free ourselves every bit as much as those who have hurt us.

Jesus elaborated on the expectation of the law:

> You have heard that it was said, "Eye for eye, and tooth for tooth." But I tell you, Do not resist an evil person. If someone strikes you on the right cheek, turn to him the other also. And if someone wants to sue you and take your tunic, let him have your cloak as well. If someone forces you to go one mile, go with him two miles. Give to the one who asks you, and do not turn away from the one who wants to borrow from you.[17]

Who could live up to that? Only the person who has accepted this fact: God's unconditional love has ended the need to decide who to forgive and who to blame. When *all* are forgiven, standards disappear and, with them, the burden of judgment. By adopting unconditional love as our single standard, we set ourselves free from heavy rocks weighing us down. But beyond that, we become more like Christ.

4. *Forgiveness is a doorway to reconciliation*

The fruit of forgiveness is always peace. Sometimes it is the inner peace we feel when we align ourselves with God's love. When we forgive, we free ourselves every bit as much as those who have hurt us. Sometimes peace flows beyond ourselves and leads to reconciliation.

Reconciliation with those who have harmed us is not always possible. It takes two to reconcile. Forgiveness is a doorway, but we do not always get to walk over its threshold. Whenever it is possible, however, reconciliation is the very heart of God.[18]

Jesus is the all-powerful Redeemer with an all-powerful love capable of forgiving anyone at anytime for any reason.

The father of the prodigal son had forgiven long before he saw the boy coming down the road. He dreamed of the restoration of their relationship. He was ready and waiting—*waiting* for that first glimpse of his son coming home, *waiting* to embrace him, *waiting* to be reconciled with him, *waiting* to see humility in him.

He hungered to see his boy, and when the day finally arrives, his hunger is finally satisfied at the sight of his son. He doesn't wait for him, he doesn't walk to him. He *runs* to meet him, full of joy, full of love, full of forgiveness. The boy deserves to be treated like a pauper, to be given a "stone," but the Father can't help but lavish love on him befitting a prince. When we let extraordinary forgiveness have its way with our hearts, even the most elusive peace is within our reach.

5. *Forgiveness erases the debt*

Divine forgiveness means that God, in His mercy, chose to release you from the penalty of your sins. If you have placed your faith in Christ Jesus and asked Him to forgive your sins, they are gone—wiped out completely. This total and permanent debt relief is available to all who choose to believe in Jesus Christ as their Lord and Savior. God says, "I will forgive their wickedness and will remember their sin no more."[19]

If all true believers understood at a heart-and-soul level how much God loves them and how Christ has freed them, everything about their existence would change for the better.

That is our challenge: to try to grasp, with our finite minds and limited comprehension, the love God lavishes upon us. If we could fully experience the magnitude of our forgiveness from God down deep at the very core of our being, we would more readily, even eagerly, grant forgiveness to others. Our hearts truly would be forever touched and warmed to *want* to forgive—it would not be a begrudging act of the will. And we'd continually be inspecting our burlap bags to make sure not even the smallest pebbles of anger, bitterness, and resentment get deposited there.

God's Forgiveness Is Forever

A pastor in the Philippines, a much-loved man of God, carried the burden of a secret sin he had committed many years before. He had repented but still had no peace, no sense of God's forgiveness.

In his church was a woman who deeply loved God and who claimed to have visions in which she spoke with Christ and He with her. The pastor, however, was skeptical. To test her, he said, "The next time you speak with Christ, I want you to ask Him what sin I committed while I was still in seminary."

The woman agreed.

A few days later, the pastor asked, "Well, did Christ visit you in your dreams?"

"Yes, He did."

"And did you ask Him what sin I committed in seminary?"

"Yes."

"Well, what did He say?"

The woman looked him straight in the eye. "He said, 'I don't remember.'"[20]

The point is well made: God forgives *and* forgets. When the Lord forgives your sins, they are gone forever. He says, "I don't remember"…and He remembers your sin no more.

Getting Rid of the Gravelly Remains

The Freedom of Full Forgiveness

One of my heroes of the faith is Corrie ten Boom, a survivor of the Nazi Holocaust and a person of astounding devotion to God. Whenever I want inspiration about the power of forgiveness, I recall her story.

In 1944, when Nazi Germany occupied Holland, an elderly watchmaker and his family were actively involved in the Dutch Underground. By hiding Jewish people in a secret room of their home, members of the ten Boom family courageously helped Jewish men, women, and children escape Hitler's roll call of death.

Yet one fateful day, their secret was discovered. A man whom Corrie's father had tutored in watchmaking a few years earlier betrayed the family and informed the Nazis of their activities. Corrie's father was arrested and sent to a concentration camp, where he soon died. Her tenderhearted sister, Betsie, also could not escape the jaws of death at the hands of her cruel captors. She perished at Ravensbruck, one of Hitler's most horrific death camps.

As for Corrie, she was also sent to Ravensbruck. There, Corrie witnessed and suffered unspeakable atrocities. Each day, she and her fellow inmates endured appalling abuse, filth, starvation, and degradation of every kind.

Unlike so many others—millions, in fact—Corrie was miraculously spared death. Because of a clerical error, she was released and walked away from the camp. What some might call coincidence or fate, Corrie called divine intervention. And because she was freed while others died, she felt a strong calling to demonstrate and declare God's love and forgiveness as often as she could.

Fast forward with me to 1947. It was two years after the war ended, and Corrie had traveled from Holland to defeated Germany with the message of God's forgiveness. The war's emotional, physical, and spiritual wounds were fresh and raw in that bitter, bombed-out land.

In a Munich church, Corrie spoke about God's love and shared her favorite mental picture regarding forgiveness. She told the audience that growing up not far from the sea, she always imagined that is where forgiven sins were thrown.

"When we confess our sins," she explained, "God casts them into the deepest ocean, gone forever.[1] And even though I cannot find a Scripture for it, I believe God then places a sign out there that says, 'No Fishing Allowed.'"

Her words were met with solemn expressions as the people who had gathered in the church stared back at her, not quite daring to believe her message of total forgiveness. She finished her talk, unaware that her own ability to forgive was about to be severely tested. She recalled what happened next:

> That's when I saw him, working his way forward against the others. One moment I saw the overcoat and the brown hat; the next, a blue uniform and a visored cap with its skull and crossbones. It came back with a rush: the huge room with its harsh overhead lights; the pathetic pile of dresses and shoes in the center of the floor; the shame of walking naked past this man. I could see my sister's frail form ahead of me, ribs sharp beneath the parchment skin. *Betsie, how thin you were!*
>
> The place was Ravensbruck, and the man who was making his way forward had been a guard—one of the most cruel guards.

Now he was in front of me, hand thrust out. "A fine message, Fraulein! How good it is to know that, as you say, all our sins are at the bottom of the sea!"

And I, who had spoken so glibly of forgiveness, fumbled in my pocketbook rather than take that hand. He would not remember me, of course—how could he remember one prisoner among those thousands of women?

But I remembered him and the leather crop swinging from his belt. I was face-to-face with one of my captors and my blood seemed to freeze.

"You mentioned Ravensbruck in your talk.... I was a guard there.... But since that time, I have become a Christian. I know that God has forgiven me for the cruel things I did there, but I would like to hear it from your lips as well. Fraulein,"—again, the hand came out—"will you forgive me?"

Corrie described her frenzy of thoughts and emotions:

I stood there—I whose sins had again and again to be forgiven—and could not forgive. Betsie had died in that place—could he erase her slow terrible death simply for the asking?

It could not have been many seconds that he stood there—hand held out—but to me it seemed hours as I wrestled with the most difficult thing I ever had to do.

For I had to do it—I knew that. The message that God forgives has a prior condition: that we forgive those who have injured us. "If you do not forgive men their trespasses," Jesus says, "neither will your Father in heaven forgive your trespasses."...And still I stood there with the coldness clutching my heart. But forgiveness is not an emotion—I knew that too. Forgiveness is an act of the will, and the will can function regardless of the temperature of the heart. "Jesus, help me!" I prayed silently. "I can lift my hand. I can do that much. You supply the feeling."

And so woodenly, mechanically, I thrust my hand into

the one stretched out to me. And as I did, an incredible thing took place. The current started in my shoulder, raced down my arm, sprang into our joined hands. And then the healing warmth seemed to flood my whole being, bringing tears to my eyes.

"I forgive you, brother!" I cried. "With all my heart!"

For a long moment, we grasped each other's hands, the former guard and the former prisoner.

Corrie later wrote, "I had never known God's love so intensely, as I did then. But even so, I realized it was not my love. I had tried, and did not have the power. It was the power of the Holy Spirit."[2]

≈

I love this story because it demonstrates how Corrie—as strong a Christian as I know—struggled mightily to forgive in the midst of sharing with thousands about the freedom of forgiveness. A mountainous boulder had been shoved deep, deep into her soul and so embedded itself there that, without the supernatural power of Christ, Corrie could not have thrown it out.

Think about it: If Corrie initially resisted, but then ultimately forgave such an egregious offender, surely there's hope for the rest of us who find forgiveness a daunting task. Corrie took steps toward forgiveness…even when she didn't *feel* like it. Her obedience chiseled away at the mountainous boulder, and with the help of the Holy Spirit it was reduced to gravelly remains that could easily be swept away. Corrie found freedom in *total* forgiveness.

Why the Difficulty of Forgiveness?

So many people I talk with *want* to forgive, and *know* they should forgive, but insist they *can't* forgive. They've accumulated so many rocks they feel there's no way they can tunnel through to freedom. Many men and women have said to me, "If you knew my situation—all the awful experiences I went through—you'd know why I can't forgive. I'm sorry, there's just no way."

Indeed, I have heard dozens of stories involving horrific abuse, and I understand why these people think it is impossible to forgive. People whose

> Forgiveness sets us free to be all God designed us to be.

lives have been damaged by cruelty and ill treatment need, most of all, sympathy, support, and love.

This brings us back to our central theme: The primary reason God wants us to forgive is because *forgiveness sets us free to be all He designed us to be.* Forgiveness is good for us as a salve on open wounds and as corrective surgery for a broken heart. Forgiveness feels good when we loosen the grip on our burdensome bag and when we rid ourselves of our rocks of resentment.

God is not a taskmaster, poking and prodding like a demanding parent, saying, "Now go on—do as you're told. Don't dilly dally. Quit sulking. Just forgive!" No, God is saying something far different. He is saying, "I care so deeply about you that I want the absolute best for you. Forgiveness is a vital way for Me to restore your joy and for you to live the abundant life I've promised you."

Barriers to Forgiveness

Even when we recognize that God has our best interests in mind, we still might insist that forgiving certain people is impossible. Why is it so difficult to forgive? Here are some of the most common barriers to forgiveness:

- *No modeling of forgiveness from parents.* "I don't know how to forgive."
- *Denying that the offense ever occurred.* "I don't want to think about it."
- *Fearing to hold the guilty accountable.* "It's really all my

fault." (This kind of thinking short-circuits the reality and the pain of being wronged.)

- *Not feeling that you can forgive yourself.* "No mercy for me, no mercy for you."

- *Not being forgiven for your past offenses.* "They didn't forgive me. Why should I forgive them?"

- *Not understanding God's forgiveness.* "God will never forgive me; I will never forgive her."

- *Believing that bitterness is a required response to betrayal.* "God knows that my feelings are normal."

- *Thinking that forgiveness excuses unjust behavior.* "I'm not about to say that what she did was okay!"

- *Requiring an apology or show of repentance.* "He shouldn't be forgiven because he's not really sorry."

- *Feeling a sense of power by hanging on to unforgiveness.* "He needs to see how wrong he is!"

- *Refusing to turn loose of revenge.* "He should pay for what he's done."

- *Harboring a prideful, hardened heart that becomes a spiritual stronghold.* "I refuse to forgive."

One or more of these rationales can block forgiveness and burden you down with stones of animosity. I've heard all the above reasons mentioned by people at one time or another, but I've heard two others so often that they warrant further explanation.

"It Wouldn't Be Fair!"

At the heart of this statement is the issue of justice. To be honest, this has been my Achilles' heel when it comes to forgiveness—always has been and probably always will be. I'm extremely justice-oriented. I want every unjust situation resolved with the utmost fairness and equality. I want criminals to be caught and punished to the full extent of the law. I want the scales of justice to balance perfectly.

I've asked myself: Why is my need for justice so strong and so natural, and why is forgiveness so difficult and so unnatural? I believe there are three reasons:

1. *God has instilled within every human heart a sense of right and wrong.* The apostle Paul pointed this out when he spoke about unbelievers (whom, in this case, he calls Gentiles) and their innate desire to follow a code of ethics or rules. "When Gentiles, who do not have the law, do by nature things required by the law...they show that the requirements of the law are written on their hearts."[3] Everyone has a God-given conscience, a sense of right and wrong. Therefore, we feel a need for justice when we are mistreated.

2. *Based on the law, forgiveness seems inappropriate.* Somehow a black-and-white, law-and-order kind of system seems controllable and quantifiable. It's neat and tidy. Consider the words of Moses: "Do to him as he intended to do to his brother. You must purge the evil from among you. The rest of the people will hear of this and be afraid, and never again will such an evil thing be done among you. Show no pity: life for life, eye for eye, tooth for tooth, hand for hand, foot for foot."[4] To a justice-oriented person like me, that sounds completely logical!

But then I come back to the very essence of Christianity, the quality that makes it different from every other religion: *grace.* Because God is a God of justice, somebody had to pay. That somebody was Jesus. The death of Jesus on the cross fulfilled the justice of God (see Romans 3:25-26).

Knowing this, should we expect justice before we extend mercy and forgiveness? Although everyone is subject to God's justice, Jesus was the payment for *each person's wrongs.* While governments mete out justice, *individually* we are to extend mercy. We are to leave *individual* justice to God. The Bible exhorts us to "be merciful, just as your Father is merciful."[5]

3. *We feel outraged when justice is denied.* Thus, the cry for justice is common from everyone—*everyone except the guilty person* waiting to receive justice. Interesting, isn't it? We demand justice when we

have been wronged—but we plead for mercy when *we* are on the hot seat. We echo the psalmist's words, "Have mercy on me, O God, according to your unfailing love; according to your great compassion blot out my transgressions."⁶ This kind of double standard—demanding justice for someone else while pleading mercy for ourselves—may be human nature, but it also sabotages a forgiving spirit.

"He Doesn't Deserve It!"

Many people believe they can't—or shouldn't have to—forgive when the offender shows no remorse or contrition. Should someone who is unwilling to apologize, or even acknowledge the wrongdoing, be granted forgiveness? That's a tough one for people who have been deeply hurt.

Joanna was listening to *Hope in the Night* one evening as I was talking about forgiveness. I mentioned that God's grace is available to *anyone* and, therefore, our willingness to forgive should not be selective or conditional.

That comment prompted a call from Joanna. "I agree with you most of the time, but I think you're wrong that we have to forgive under *any* circumstance. Some people just don't deserve it."

Joanna came to that conclusion because of her childhood with an abusive father. His offenses against her spanned the entire spectrum: psychological, emotional, and physical. She had been in such unrelenting pain that she'd attempted suicide while in college.

Some time after that, she had become a Christian and joined a church support group for victims of abuse. As time passed, she saw the need to forgive her father and made real progress in giving her past to God. Every day, she felt stronger and more at peace. Finally, she decided the time had come to face her father again and to tell him she had forgiven him. The results?

"He just laughed at me. He swore and told me he had nothing to be sorry for. In fact, he said *I* should apologize to *him* for putting him through the hell of raising me. Even when I tried to forgive him, he humiliated me, just like he did so many times growing up."

Joanna's resolve to forgive went out the window. The cumulative weight of a lifetime of pain and anger came crashing down on her. It was as if her bulging bag of boulders had fallen squarely on her chest, knocking all the air out of her.

> On the cross, Jesus prayed, "Father, forgive them," even though no one said, "I'm sorry."

"I decided then and there that I would never forgive him until he asked for it," she said with rock-hard determination. A situation like Joanna's puts the issue of forgiveness in the crucible—where lofty thoughts meet the earthly reality of suffering.

Why Did Jesus Forgive?

Of all the horrendous offenses in history, none compares with what human beings did to Jesus on the day of His crucifixion. They beat Him, mocked Him, and humiliated Him. They executed Him in the cruelest possible way. No one has ever been as blameless or suffered as much as Jesus did that day. Yet in His death He modeled how to forgive our offenders—even when regret or remorse hasn't been expressed.

The proof is in Jesus' prayer as He hung on the cross. "Father, forgive them, for they do not know what they are doing."[7] No one had asked to be forgiven. No one had shown remorse. No one said, "I'm sorry." As Jesus' words show, they were not even aware of the unthinkable crime they were committing—killing Christ, the Son of God. Yet He forgave them…and in the process, He forgave us.[8]

Some people have wondered: "When Jesus was on the cross, He prayed, 'Father, forgive them.' Does that mean that everyone present at Jesus' crucifixion received salvation?" No. Realize that forgiveness is a gift and the forgiver is blessed in giving the gift whether the person offered the gift is willing to receive it or not. Many refuse forgiveness because accepting it requires acknowledging the need of it.

Being offered a gift is one matter, receiving the gift is another. Having your sins paid for by Jesus is one matter. Receiving and benefiting from His payment is another.

It is our part to give forgiveness and it is the offender's part to receive forgiveness.

As I talked this through with Joanna, I pointed out that Jesus' motive was not fairness or justice. He prayed for the Father to extend mercy to those who wronged Him because of His extraordinary love. The only way we can forgive others who harm and steal part of our lives is because Jesus said, "Father, forgive them." Of course He didn't mean that they were unaware of their actions; rather, they

Sculpting a Masterpiece

Marble comes from a quarry, often in large blocks and slabs. When a sculptor needs marble, he submits the size specifications of the piece he needs (the length, width, thickness, and shape), and he will also address other factors, such as color, grain, finish, and pattern.

Massive blocks of marble aren't easily removed, just as the one who severely wounds isn't easily forgiven. It can be a painstaking process when the burdens are especially heavy, and complete forgiveness can take significant time.

But when you yield those overbearing blocks that are weighing you down, presenting them to the Master Sculptor, He will create an unexpected masterpiece. He will carefully chisel away everything that does not conform you to the character of Christ.

By God's grace and in His time, you will truly be able to forgive offenses even as large as a mammoth slab of marble. He will hoist away the heaviest hurt—that burden you thought you would always bear—but will use the experience to mold you, to sculpt you into a masterpiece... far beyond the imagination of even Michelangelo.

couldn't see beyond their noses to the ramifications of their actions. They were spiritually deaf, dumb, and blind! Christ's extraordinary love—His *agape* love (seeking what is best for another person)—is the only means by which we are empowered to forgive those who have plunged a knife in our heart or a spear in our side.

Christ suffered unjustly and horrendously for the forgiveness of our sins—yours, mine, and everyone else's.[9] Therefore, if you are a true Christian, you can rely on Christ (who lives in you) to enable you to endure unjust suffering...but even more so, to forgive those who mistreat you.

Be clear about this point: Every Christian is called to suffer, but with that suffering comes a blessing. As the apostle Peter wrote, "This is commendable before God. To this you were called, because Christ suffered for you, leaving you an example, that you should follow in his steps....When they hurled their insults at him, he did not retaliate; when he suffered, he made no threats. Instead, he *entrusted himself to him who judges justly.*"[10]

Why Let Them Off the Hook?

If you've ever dug in your heels on the issue of forgiveness, it's likely you've thought something like this: *I'm supposed to just let her off the hook? I suffer while she gets off scot-free? I don't think so!*

You need to understand that forgiveness is not a matter of letting the offender off the hook. It is a matter of taking the wrongdoer off *your* hook and placing that person onto *God's* hook. There's a phrase in 1 Peter 2:23 that is crucial in empowering us to forgive: Jesus "entrusted himself to him who judges justly."

The Lord wants you to take your pain from the past and release it into His hands. Realize this key concept:

- *"It is mine to avenge; I will repay.* In due time their foot will slip; their day of disaster is near and their doom rushes upon them."[11]

- "Will not God bring about justice for his chosen ones, who cry out to him day and night? Will he keep putting them off? I tell you, *he will see that they get justice, and quickly.*"[12]

Passages such as these satisfy our need for justice and fairness while removing the burden from our shoulders. God will deal with each person according to his or her deeds.

This concept enabled Joanna to forgive her father, even though he refused to take responsibility for the pain he caused. No matter what he says to her, God will deal with him justly and call him to account, either in this life or the next. With this realization, Joanna was freed to forgive her father.

After removing herself from this rocky relationship, Joanna moved on with her life, assured that God was completely in control of the situation. She had to bore through layer after layer of painful memories that served as obstacles to finding the rich reward of forgiveness—freedom. But her obedience and fresh understanding of God's justice helped grind away a lifetime of bitterness to find her breakthrough in *total forgiveness*.

How Many Times Should I Grant Mercy?

Do you remember when Peter asked Jesus if he should forgive a person seven times? (see Matthew 18:21). I think Peter was quite proud of himself saying *seven* times—not just two, three, or four! Peter was being most generous. Do you recall how Jesus answered?

"I do not say to you, up to seven times, but up to seventy times seven" (Matthew 18:22 NKJV).

Wow—no one could have expected this response! And the point is not to count, *Oh, this is offense #3...this is #13...this is #43.* No doubt this response elicited more than a few raised eyebrows. Jesus' point was that we are to forgive *whenever* there is an offense—*no matter how many times.*

Knowing human nature and our propensity to withhold forgiveness, Jesus tells a simple story to drive home His point. A servant owes the king 10,000 talents (about $50,000,000 in today's currency). The king orders the servant and his family be sold—literally—along with all they have in order to make restitution.

The servant falls on his knees begging for mercy, "Have patience with me, and I will pay you everything."

The king extends mercy and forgives the entire debt.

Later, this same servant grabs a fellow servant who owes him 100 denarii (about $50). He begins to choke him and demand repayment. His fellow servant falls to his knees begging for mercy.

"Have patience with me," the desperate man cries, "and I will pay you everything."

But the first servant refuses and has the man thrown into prison until he can pay the debt.

When the other servants see this happen, they are greatly distressed and tell the king. The cruel servant is called before the king, who is angry that the servant had not extended the same mercy he had received.

"You wicked servant!" the king says. "I forgave you all your debt because you pleaded with me. Shouldn't you have had mercy on your fellow servant just as I had mercy on you?"

In his anger, the king throws the unmerciful servant back into jail until he can pay all he owes.

Jesus concludes the story by saying, "This is how my heavenly Father will treat each of you unless you forgive your brother from your heart."[13]

The king in this parable represents God, who forgives all our debt of sin when we come to Him sincerely for forgiveness and mercy. The servant who has his debts removed but is unwilling to forgive the debts of another servant has his debt reinstated, which he now has to pay in full. Likewise, if we do not extend true forgiveness to others, we forfeit the blessings that come with God's forgiveness of us. When we lug around a rock-filled bag of resentment by withholding forgiveness, God holds back the blessings He has in store for us.

One of the major reasons people struggle to forgive is because they do not fully understand that the Greek word *charizomai*, which is translated "forgive," means to "bestow a favor *unconditionally*." The Greek word *charis* means "grace," which is "giving a gift that is not deserved." Forgiveness is based on grace and is an expression of grace. Therefore, you are an expression of God's grace when you forgive others. When you forgive someone, you multiply the grace of God. Paul echoed this sentiment when he told the Ephesians, "Be kind and compassionate to one another, forgiving each other, *just as in Christ God forgave you*" (4:32). When we truly understand how much we've been forgiven by our heavenly Father, we will not fail to extend that same forgiveness to others.

> When you forgive, you multiply the grace of God.

What Are the Risks and Rewards of Forgiveness?
The Risks

With Jesus, forgiveness is black and white—there is no gray. He clearly states, "If you forgive men when they sin against you, your heavenly Father will also forgive you. But if you do not forgive men their sins, your Father will not forgive your sins."[14] Obviously, the consequence of choosing not to forgive is *huge*.

Refusing to forgive can be a block to salvation

Bill, who had been coming to my home Bible study, said he was puzzled: "I've prayed the prayer of salvation several times, but I know I'm not saved." First I made sure he understood God's plan of salvation, which he did. Then after again praying for Christ to come into his life, he said with frustration, "I still know I'm not saved."

I paused, asking God to reveal the *real* problem. All of a sudden, a question flashed into my mind: "Bill, is there anyone you refuse to forgive?" Immediately, his calm countenance changed. With a scowling face, tight jaw, and squinting eyes, he answered "Yes—my ex-wife! And *she doesn't deserve* to be forgiven!"

After hearing his litany of offenses, I explained, "Bill, becoming an authentic Christian means receiving Jesus Christ as *Lord* and Savior. The Bible says, 'Believe in [rely upon] the *Lord* Jesus Christ and you will be saved.'"[15]

"If He is truly your Lord, that means He is your master, ruler, owner—to whom you yield your will to His. If He says forgive, you must be willing to forgive. If you refuse to forgive, you are still being your own ruler. You are not receiving Him as your Lord."

Quickly he responded, "I can't."

"Bill, God would never tell you to do something without giving you the power to do it."

"I just can't—no! I won't." Bill walked away still carrying a bulging bag of bitterness…and I never saw him again.

About four months later at a conference in California, I was approached by a female version of Bill. Brenda had been dumped by her husband—dumped for a much younger woman.

Although she too had previously prayed asking Jesus to come into her life, she felt as though there were a stone wall around her soul, blocking her from salvation. I asked her the same question I had posed to Bill: "Is there anyone you have refused to forgive?"

"Yes—and this is why…," detailing her feelings as a "dumpee"— the betrayal, humiliation, disbelief. Again, I shared the matter-of-fact passage spoken by Jesus.

Brenda's immediate response was, "Oh! I didn't know that. Obviously I *must* forgive him." And sure enough, I led Brenda in a prayer in which she told the Lord that she was willing to forgive. She took all her boulders of bitterness off of her emotional hook and placed them all onto God's hook, and she released her husband in the same way. Then she asked the Lord's forgiveness for all her sins and genuinely received Jesus as her personal Savior and Lord.

At the end of our time together, both tears of joy and the peace of God visibly transformed her face!

What a *risk* Bill took—what a *reward* Brenda received!

Refusing to forgive can be a block to God's blessings

Unforgiveness affects our fellowship with God and others, and the bestowing of blessings. *All* our sins were already forgiven at the moment of salvation. Does this mean true Christians can lose their salvation if they keep holding onto rocks of resentment and refuse to forgive? The answer is no. Romans 8:1 states, "There is now *no condemnation* for those who are in Christ Jesus."

Once we are adopted into the family of Christ, there is no condemnation. That means *no condemnation*! Additionally, once we become true Christians, the Bible says we are given *eternal life*. And just how long is eternal?[16] Eternal is *eternal*—that means forever! So, how can we lose a gift that God says is eternal? We can't.

What then does this scripture mean for Christians—that the Father won't forgive us if we refuse to forgive? One of the Greek words translated "forgive" means "lift off, send away, release." Simply put, when we refuse to forgive others, the weight of resentment, the rocks of revenge, the stones of scorn are *not lifted off*—neither are we released from the pressure of a heavy heart nor are we free from the burden of bitterness. On top of that, we build a barrier that blocks the blessings of God. And saddest of all, we grieve the heart of God (see Appendix A on page 195).

The choice is ours: We can be stuck with our stones of resentment, or we can be free to run with forgiveness.

Thankfully, there's a flip side to this cause-and-effect equation: He lavishes blessings on those who do show forgiveness and mercy. I love the language Jesus used when He said, "Do not judge, and you will not be judged. Do not condemn, and you will not be condemned. *Forgive, and you will be forgiven.* Give, and it will be given to you. A good measure, pressed down, shaken together and running over, will be poured into your lap. For with the measure you use, it will be measured to you."[17]

Whatever God determines that "good measure" to be for *you*— be it wisdom, meaningful work, special relationships—it's sure to bless your life. When we offer love, mercy, and forgiveness to others, it will be returned to us measure for measure. If we're generous with our kindness toward other people, God will return that to us so that it's "running over."

The Rewards

Let's look at some of the specific blessings we can receive when we choose to extend forgiveness to others:

Forgiveness opens the door to God's forgiveness. "If you forgive men when they sin against you, your heavenly Father will also forgive you."[18]

Forgiveness prevents a root of bitterness from growing. "See to it that no one misses the grace of God and that no bitter root grows up to cause trouble and defile many."[19]

Forgiveness closes a door to Satan in our lives. "What I have forgiven—if there was anything to forgive—I have forgiven in the sight of Christ for your sake, in order that Satan might not outwit us. For we are not unaware of his schemes."[20]

> When we forgive as we have been forgiven, we give the kind of mercy that can change the hearts of others.

Forgiveness brings us into the light. "Anyone who claims to be in the light but hates his brother is still in the darkness. Whoever loves his brother lives in the light, and there is nothing in him to make him stumble."[21]

Forgiveness reflects a godly heart. "The godless in heart harbor resentment."[22]

Forgiveness gets us in sync with the Spirit of God. "Do not grieve the Holy Spirit of God.... Get rid of all bitterness, rage and anger, brawling and slander, along with every form of malice."[23]

≈

Forgiveness Leads to Blessings

Good things come into our lives when we choose to follow in Jesus' footsteps of grace. When we *choose* to follow—which means forgiving even when we don't feel like it.

When we forgive as we have been forgiven, we demonstrate the kind of love and mercy that changes hearts and changes the world. We can turn loose of that heavy bag of bitterness we've been holding onto so tightly—*and be blessed!* And when we extend total forgiveness, the gravelly remains are gone. Not a speck of sand can be spotted.

When Corrie ten Boom stood face-to-face with the former Nazi prison guard, why could she not extend her hand? It was as though a two-ton boulder of bitterness were weighing her arm down, totally immobilizing it. When it comes to forgiving someone who has wronged us, we might resist—like Corrie resisted. But through the power of the Spirit and the recognition of our own redemption, we can go on to extend our hand and say, "I forgive you, brother, with all my heart!"

Removing Hard Rocks of Resentment

Choosing Forgiveness over Feelings

CLARA BARTON, THE FOUNDER OF the American Red Cross, was reminded by a friend one day of a vicious deed someone had done to her years before. Clara had been deeply wounded by the incident. But when it was brought to her attention, she acted as if she was completely unaware of the hurtful attack.

"Don't you remember it?" her friend asked.

"No," Clara replied and paused. "I distinctly remember forgetting it."

All of us struggling with forgiveness need to burn this phrase into our minds: *I distinctly remember forgetting it.*

Is Forgiveness Always a Choice?

In the course of talking about forgiveness with hundreds of hurting people over the years, I've heard countless stories of abuse, injustice, and betrayal. People have described to me the deep wounds piercing their hearts. The injuries they've suffered span the entire spectrum of evil that people are capable of inflicting on one another.

Night after night, I listen to people in pain: victims of physical, verbal, and emotional abuse: survivors of sexual abuse; men and women in the throes of divorce; devastating stories of infidelity, pornography, financial ruin; parents who relive the nightmare of a child killed by a drunk driver; children who disclose the pain of divorce, alcoholism, abandonment; teens who struggle with peer pressure over sex, gangs, drugs; entire families that agonize over substance abuse, gambling, sex, pregnancies, abortion, and broken relationships.

Even seemingly less traumatic events—cruel words by a once-trusted confidant, embezzlement by a once-trusted employee, rejection by a once-trusted friend—cause pain that can haunt for years. Clearly, not a single person on earth is immune from deep hurt and heartache.

Still, that doesn't mean we have to stay forever distressed, devastated by the destructive behavior that wrought such pain in our lives. We must remind ourselves, for our good, and for the good of others, that *forgiveness is not a feeling*. Indeed, forgiveness is a purposeful decision—an act of the will not dependent on our emotions. No matter what has been done to us, or how badly it hurts, we must forgive because of this inescapable and profound truth: *God has forgiven us all the more.*

Aren't you grateful God is not gleefully piling up a bag full of offenses with your name on it?

What Part Does Feeling Play in Forgiving?

Does forgiving another person mean we are to ignore, hide, or bury our pain? Absolutely not. To say that forgiveness is not a feeling in no way implies that the painful emotions we experience are unjustified, unnatural, or "un-Christian." In fact, it's safe to say that forgiveness always begins with pain. After all, Christlike forgiveness would be unnecessary if there were no injury by another person. Pain is a message to us that something is wrong—*pain gets our attention.*

The raw emotion of profound pain is what causes people to think...

- *It hurts much too much. There's no way I could forgive her!*

- *I feel so much anger. I could never forgive him!*
- *In my head I want to forgive, but in my heart there's too much rage.*

Thoughts like these are all too common—sincere thoughts from those who have been wounded. But what these people fail to grasp is this: *Pain should never stand in the way of forgiveness.*

God does not ask us to deny our pain. He understands sadness and sorrow. He feels the weight of our hearts—the heaviness—even more than we

> Forgiveness is more powerful than the most overwhelming pain.

do. What else can we conclude from the fact that God loved the world so much that He willingly sent His only Son to die on the cross for our sins so that we could have eternal life?[1]

By sacrificing His life, Jesus displayed the truth that *forgiveness is far more powerful than the most overwhelming pain*. In fact, forgiveness is the only real remedy for our rocks of resentment, revenge, and anger—all the emotions that batter us after we have been betrayed. By following Jesus' example, we choose healing instead of hatred, and we refuse to drag around our bulging bag of bitterness. And to possess this healing, we must face the pain, not deny or suppress it.

How can I say that forgiveness is not a feeling? If our feelings of pain should not be ignored, then what does it mean that forgiveness is a decision—an act of the will? We must understand that our emotions—however powerful and persistent—are the least reliable measures of truth. Feelings can be miserably misleading. Feelings are influenced by numerous conditions both past and present that can have nothing to do with reality.

Being *aware* of our emotions is one matter, and giving them *control* is quite another, for at least three reasons:

- Feelings cannot be trusted to give us a clear picture of what is true about our lives.

- Feelings fluctuate from one minute to the next, often without reason.

- Feelings are far too subjective for us to put our faith in them.

Most of us have had the experience of going to bed feeling mad at someone, only to wake up completely unable to remember why we were mad to begin with. *Why was I so angry?* we ask ourselves. *It wasn't that big a deal.* Well, sometimes feelings blatantly lead us astray.

Suppose you pass by one friend and exchange smiles and hellos. Then a second friend scowls and walks by without a word. The rest of the day you stew and simmer, reaching the boiling point emotionally. *How rude! What's the matter with her?* But then you think, *Maybe I did something to offend her.* Later, when you muster the courage to confront her, she says, "What? This morning? Oh, I'm sorry—I didn't even see you. I was still fuming about a phone call."

Oops. False alarm.

Something so critical and central to a victorious Christian life as forgiveness cannot possibly depend on ever-changing emotions. Forgiveness is a decisive act of the will—*a fight for control of how we think.* When we are wronged, of course it will hurt. Of course we will feel angry. Of course we will want justice. These are feelings that can naturally arise when someone offends us.

What Part Does Thinking Play in Forgiving?

While God does not ask us to stifle or bury our pain, He does ask that we *change how we think* about those who have harmed us. This is good news for anyone struggling to forgive. By sacrificing His Son as payment for our sins—even when we did not deserve it—God gave us a *new way of thinking* that has the power to loosen the stranglehold our emotions have on us. As the apostle Paul said, "Do not conform any longer to the pattern of this world, but be transformed by the renewing of your mind. Then you will be able to test and approve what God's will is—his good, pleasing and perfect will."[2] We renew our minds by *learning to think like God thinks.*

The old way of thinking went like this: Anyone who broke God's law had to be punished—period. That is why the Pharisees felt justified at dragging the adulterous woman in front of Jesus and demanding she be condemned to death. The old thinking about judgment was a bedrock for their *feelings* of righteous indignation and outrage.

When Jesus died for us, however, He ushered in a whole new way for us to relate to one another. If God forgave *our* debt and freed us from a sentence of death, what right do we have to demand payment from *others?* If we refuse to forgive, we become a higher judge than God Himself!

The Bible says, "There is now no condemnation for those who are in Christ Jesus."[3] If we believe this, how can we continue to condemn others, as if God's grace had never been seen within Jesus and made alive by Jesus and come to us through Jesus? We forgive not because it feels right, but because we doggedly decide to follow Christ's example. We forgive because we choose to, and we do it right in the very midst of our pain.

We systematically begin removing every rancorous rock, every spiteful stone, and every bitter boulder from the bag of our soul.

But that picture is still incomplete. By requiring us to forgive, no matter how we feel, God has presented us with a daunting task that takes discipline and self-sacrifice. Forgiving our offender does not come naturally. To succeed, we must want to follow God more than we want to follow our feelings—our feelings of revenge, that power play called "get even."

But, as usual, alongside the challenge God has set before us, He provides a promise: "In all things God works for the good of those who love him, who have been called according to his purpose."[4] Here we are given a poignant new way of thinking about our own pain—one that sets us free to trust God completely.

What Is God's Role After We Forgive?

Simply put, this striking promise from God assures us that even when we have suffered a terrible wound, things are not always as they appear. *Pain is not without purpose.* Pain is a catalyst for "the good of those who...have been called according to His *purpose.*"

As in the making of a diamond, time, heat, and pressure all work to produce a rock of magnificent beauty. Our loving God sees every one of us as diamonds in the rough, allowing these same three components to work in our lives to transform us from a dirty lump of coal to a dazzling rock, a diamond that shines for the glory of God!

God calls Himself a refiner. Our Refiner uses fiery tests and trials to remove the dross from our lives—yes, that scummy surface gunk that gets in the way of developing sterling character. Isaiah 48:10 conveys the link between pain and purification: "Behold, I have refined you, but not as silver; I have tried you in the furnace of affliction."[5]

He refines, and He cleanses, "for he is like a refiner's fire.... He will sit as a refiner and purifier of silver, and he will purify the sons of Levi and refine them like gold and silver."[6]

From Pain to Fame: Joseph's Story

No one better expresses the purpose of pain than Joseph, whose story in found in the book of Genesis.[7] No one had a greater "right" to be resentful than Joseph. He endured one betrayal after another, beginning the day his brothers threw him into an empty, dry pit and then sold him like an animal to slave merchants headed for Egypt. In an instant, he went from being on top of the world as father's favorite son to looking up from the bottom of a pit in the middle of the desert.

It's when Joseph openly shares his dreams—in which his parents and all his brothers bow down to him—that his brothers become jealous. Perhaps they were afraid that he, a younger brother, would usurp the blessings that should go to them as older brothers. It didn't help that their father favored Joseph over the other sons. Whatever the case, he didn't deserve the treatment he got from them.

Who knows how long Joseph struggles to let go of the past and accept his new status in life. In Egypt, he is now simply a slave—the property of a man named Potiphar. But the Bible reveals "the Lord was with him," and he quickly becomes the most trusted servant in Potiphar's house. As a result, he is put in charge of everything his master owns.

If the story ended there, we might say it did not turn out so badly for Joseph. Things certainly could have been worse. But unfortunately for Joseph, his master's wife is attracted to the handsome young Hebrew and pressures him to have sex with her. He repeatedly refuses, not wanting to sin against God, nor to repay with such treachery the trust he has been given. Potiphar's wife, feeling scorned, falsely accuses Joseph of trying to seduce her. Potiphar, a captain in Pharaoh's army, promptly throws Joseph into prison.

Injustice again follows Joseph to his new circumstance. Life in an Egyptian prison probably makes both the desert pit and slavery seem appealing. Though he had already fallen far—from favored son to slave—he learns he still has farther to fall: from slave to prisoner, with little hope of mercy. His cell walls could echo with understandably angry words against God and against all who have treated him unfairly. But the Bible says, "The LORD was with Joseph and showed him steadfast love and gave him favor in the sight of the keeper of the prison."[8] Again Joseph is given the highest trust and responsibility.

One day, Joseph overhears two fellow inmates talking about their dreams, curious to know what they mean. Joseph's past experience with interpreting his dreams to his brothers could have caused him to keep his mouth shut. But rather he says to his fellow prisoners, the former baker and cupbearer from Pharaoh's court, "Do not interpretations belong to God? Please tell them to me."[9] Afterward, Joseph divulges what the dreams mean: The cupbearer will be restored to his position in Pharaoh's court, and the baker will be hanged.

Joseph then asks the cupbearer, who will return to the palace, to put in a good word for him with Pharaoh. Probably the man promises to do so as he joyfully leaves the prison three days later. But once outside the prison walls, the now-free cupbearer fails Joseph. Two years pass before he thinks about Joseph again.

By this time betrayal and disappointment are commonplace occurrences in Joseph's life. Each day Joseph could have cursed God for allowing him to be unjustly imprisoned. He could have accused God of teasing him with such a rare opportunity to get a fair hearing from Pharaoh, only to have it slip away. He could have resented his former cellmate for not returning his kindness. How many months go by before Joseph gives up hope for his release? For most of us, hope would have given way to despair. But Joseph simply keeps his trust in God and keeps a trustworthy walk of integrity. God has a plan and, though Joseph could never have imagined where he would eventually end up, it is enough for him to have faith in the future God has and obey Him right where he is.

When it is Pharaoh's turn to have a pair of puzzling dreams—scenes his advisors can't decipher—the cupbearer finally remembers Joseph and tells his story to Pharaoh. Joseph, summoned from the prison to the palace, listens to Pharaoh's dreams and warns him that God intends to send seven years of famine, but only after seven years of good harvests. He advises Pharaoh to choose a trustworthy man to oversee storing as much food as possible during the years of plenty so that Egypt can survive the famine. Pharaoh chooses Joseph to be that man, and he becomes governor of all Egypt, rising much higher than he had fallen through the years of injustice, betrayal, and suffering.

If this were a Hollywood movie script, the music might reach a crescendo and the credits start to roll in this proverbial feel-good, rags-to-riches story. But God's plan to show us that "all things work together for good" is only just beginning. The famine that God reveals in Pharaoh's dreams is not limited to Egypt. It strikes Joseph's former homeland as well.

The brothers who had betrayed him so horribly all those many years ago now come to Egypt seeking food. They stand before Joseph in desperate need—*without recognizing him*. They bow before him and humbly ask his permission to buy grain that would feed their family—the family Joseph had long been separated from.

Most of us, relishing the idea of retaliation and revenge, would probably tell them to get back on their camels and hit the road...or worse. Joseph, however, is a man of God and understands from the beginning that vengeance belongs to God alone. He also knows that great good can come from great injustice. When his chance comes to punish his brothers, he does what God asks us all to do: forgive. Finally, revealing himself to his brothers, he says:

> Do not be distressed and do not be angry with yourselves for selling me here, because it was to save lives that God sent me ahead of you. For two years now there has been famine in the land, and for the next five years there will not be plowing and reaping. But God sent me ahead of you to preserve for you a remnant on earth and to save your lives by a great deliverance. So then, it was not you who sent me here, but God. He made me father to Pharaoh, lord of his entire household and ruler of all Egypt.[10]

How remarkable that, after all Joseph has been through, his first thought is for *his brothers,* not himself. He could easily say, "Now listen, just because things appear to have worked out okay and I've got this plum position at the palace, don't think I've forgotten how badly it hurt to watch you ride off in the desert and leave me in the hands of thieves and slave traders. You have no idea how much pain that caused! I hope you rot in prison!"

But that is not what he says. His words express the opposite sentiment: "Do not be distressed and do not be angry with yourselves for selling me here..." In this statement, we see that Joseph had long ago forgiven his brothers and released them from the debt he held against them. That debt had vanished so completely that

Joseph is worried that his brothers will blame themselves unnecessarily.

What Did Joseph Know in Order to Forgive?

Can we learn something from Joseph's story about our own struggle to forgive, or was he just an extraordinarily forgiving man? I believe the answer is this: Through his many years as a slave and a prisoner, Joseph had learned to entrust himself to God and master his thoughts. He had learned to walk by faith, not allowing his emotions to sway him. He could do this because deep in his heart he knew three powerful truths.

1. *Joseph knew God is sovereign*

Joseph accepts that his life belongs to God and that nothing happens apart from His will. When we truly believe this, there can

---

To Shape...Not to Shatter

Malachite is a semiprecious stone of silky banded beauty with varied hues of velvety green. Though prone to *shatter under pressure*, this valuable stone still fascinates those who otherwise fret over its fragility.

Likewise, the *pressure of painful offenses* can make you feel emotionally fragile, as if you are on the verge of shattering. And such offenses can fuel the heat of resentment. In the same way that fire can reduce malachite to raw copper—its beauty lost, its value diminished— the seething heat of resentment can damage your relationships and destroy your peace.

But when you give your resentful rocks to the Master Craftsman, He will transform every trial into a treasured opportunity to become more like Him and to display His heart to a world that has no hope. Make no mistake, your pain has a purpose...always intended to *shape* you, not to *shatter* you.

be no real injustice. "Do not be distressed and do not be angry with yourselves for selling me here," Joseph said, for "God sent me." Joseph tells his brothers that God's plan always trumps people's selfish and hurtful intentions. Therefore, hard rocks of resentment were never harbored.

> We may not know why God sends us to a place of pain, but we can know that He always has a purpose.

When we fully accept that God is sovereign, then no matter where we are or what happens to us along the way, we will have an attitude of forgiveness toward those who cause us pain. We will see them as instruments in God's hand to achieve His purposes.

2. *Joseph knew that within God's will, suffering has a purpose*

"God sent me before you to preserve life,"[11] Joseph tells his brothers. In that moment, all the pain of abandonment and betrayal he had felt in years of captivity is nothing compared with the joy of seeing God's plan to save his family unfold before his eyes. "God sent me before you to preserve for you a remnant on earth, and to keep alive for you many survivors. So it was not you who sent me here, but God."[12]

When we decide to believe that "all things work together for good," we will have an attitude of forgiveness, for we can no longer see our suffering as pointless. We may not always know why God sends us to a place of adversity (physically or emotionally), but we can trust that He always has a purpose and His purpose is always to do good. But part of that purpose, or plan, *never* calls for any of us to pick up a bag and stockpile rocks, stones, and boulders. The Bible describes the refining process by our Refiner in this way: "Remove the dross from the silver, and out comes material for the silversmith."[13]

3. *Joseph knew that God delights in turning evil into good*

The story of Joseph is a thrill ride that has more twists and turns than the most spellbinding novel—but the best is yet to come. It turns out that after Joseph reassures his brothers that he is not holding a grudge against them, he brings his entire family to Egypt to provide for them. Sometime after they all settle into their new land, Joseph's beloved father, Jacob, dies.

Even after all Joseph had done for his brothers, they still wonder if his forgiveness is genuine. "When Joseph's brothers saw that their father was dead, they said, 'What if Joseph holds a grudge against us and pays us back for all the wrongs we did to him?' "[14] So they send him a message via servants that says, "Your father left these instructions before he died."[15] In other words, your father, whom you loved so much, really wanted you to forgive us and do us no harm.

Then the brothers came to Joseph and bowed down before him, saying, "We are your slaves." Joseph delivers another astounding reply: "You meant evil against me, but God meant it for good."[16] That belief no doubt sustained him through many excruciating years of injustice.

Those words and that truth can sustain you as well. In the midst of pain, you probably can't see the good, only the evil. But God is at work orchestrating events to turn a bleak situation into a beautiful one. That same God who intervened in Joseph's life is intervening in yours, even if you perceive no evidence of that right now. He is arranging, coordinating, and synchronizing details in your life so that evil will be transformed into good, and He will use all that heat and pressure over time to enable you to shine like a diamond!

≈

God Intended It for Good

How can we echo Clara Barton's phrase and say, "I distinctly remember forgetting that"? We have these two phrases from the

Bible to empower us to see beyond any offense against us and glimpse a blessing ahead:

- "You intended to harm me, but God intended it for good."[17]
- "All things work together for good, for those who are called according to His purpose."[18]

When we hold tightly to these truths, we can choose to show love instead of hate…give grace instead of law…extend forgiveness instead of holding a grudge. We can choose to acknowledge God's sovereignty over our lives and believe in His genuine joy at turning evil into good. We can choose to think like God thinks; we can forgive as He forgives us.

CUTTING THE BOTTOM OUT OF THE BAG

Resentful Thoughts Released, Not Rehearsed

WHEN MARSHA CALLED *Hope in the Night*, her voice quickly revealed she was desperate and distraught.

As she told her story, I instantly understood the reason for the intensity of her anger and pain. Her 12-year-old daughter had been sexually violated. Misty had been molested repeatedly over a period of many months—in her own home. To make matters worse, the perpetrator of this insidious crime was Marsha's younger brother, who was living with her family while in college.

At the time of the call, it had been a year since Marsha learned of the abuse. "For the first few months, I just went numb. I felt like a hollow robot as we worked through a maze of police interviews... sworn statements...abuse counselors for my daughter. I was afraid to let myself feel anything or I would be crushed by the weight of it all."

Who could blame her? Marsha was mentally, emotionally, and spiritually devastated. Hers was a heavy bag of multiple burdens— boulder-sized burdens no mother should ever have to bear. She wrestled with her daughter's wounds as the victim of a terrible crime. She grappled with her own guilt at "failing" to see the signs that something was not right. She endured the shocking outrage of her own brother being the betrayer. She struggled with a toxic combination of justice and guilt—justice on behalf of her daughter and guilt over her brother's incarceration. Oh, yes...and she seethed with anger at family members who took her brother's "side"—those who refused to acknowledge his guilt.

Together these stones of exasperation stretched her emotional bag almost beyond capacity.

Marsha poured out her heart, pausing frequently to collect herself and contain the mixture of emotional extremes that threatened to overwhelm her.

"I'm just hanging on by a thread. And the one thin thread that's keeping me from going over the edge is my faith in God. Of course I'm angry that He would allow this to happen, but I believe by faith that He can see us through it."

After we talked for a long time and prayed together, I encouraged her to call back whenever she needed support.

A few months later, Marsha did call again with a progress report. Her daughter was doing well in therapy. Her family had taken steps to reconcile. Her brother had been sentenced to prison, but he was also enrolled in a treatment program. They had all weathered the storm—at least the worst of the storm—and were slowly returning to relative peace. They were battered, but not irreparably broken.

Everyone, that is, except Marsha. For her, the process of healing had been like anesthesia wearing off after major surgery.

"All the pain comes roaring back when I least expect it." She spoke in a wrung-out tone. "I have tried to forgive him. I know that's what God wants me to do, but I don't think I can. I don't think I'll ever be able to. I can't get the graphic images out of my mind."

I assured Marsha that all of us start at the same place on the road to forgiveness: *in heavy pain*. We all think the journey is too long, up a mountain too high, with a backpack too big. But I reminded her that none of us ever faces the task of forgiveness alone. God doesn't demand that we forgive, then leave us struggling to try to find strength. His grace—giving us strength we don't possess—is an ever-present help along the way. As the Bible says, "He gives power to the weak."[1]

Then I asked Marsha about her last comment regarding her inability to get the graphic images out of her mind.

"No matter what I do, with no provocation whatsoever, my mind is flooded with scenes of what it must have been like for my daughter. I see it all in vivid detail. With all my rage, I can't help but imagine myself beating him off of her. I can't turn it off. The images haunt me all the time."

Marsha had a blockade—a huge mound of boulders blocking her ability to forgive her brother—a blockade built *by her own thoughts*. I gently pointed out expressions of helplessness and passivity. It showed in her words, "No matter what I do... I can't help but imagine... I can't turn it off."

> Changing course is hard, and it takes deliberate efforts and repetition to make it happen.

Marsha mistakenly believed that her pain and rage blocked her ability to forgive. Instead, her unchecked thoughts were the boulders that kept piling up and producing landslides of negative thoughts she desperately needed to stop.

Since forgiveness is not a feeling but a purposeful *choice*, learning to forgive is not a matter of doing what *feels* right. Forgiveness is a decision, a matter of doggedly deciding to follow the Lord's example—and His command—to release our resentment toward those who have wronged us. To do that, we must change how we think.

I know the objection: "Sure, that sounds good...but a lot easier said than done!" And that's right—it isn't easy. *How we think* about forgiveness is deeply ingrained. Our thoughts are like covered wagons that have traveled the same road over and over across the prairie of our minds, leaving deep ruts. Changing course is hard and it takes deliberate efforts and repetition to make it happen.

Are You the Master of Your Mind?

Thoughts have great power to shape our lives. Ralph Waldo

Emerson rightly observed, "A man is what he thinks about all day long." Perhaps he was echoing the proverb that says, "For as [a man] thinks in his heart, so is he."[2]

Some thoughts are constructive and serve as a catalyst for change. Others are destructive and destroy our hope for healing. Perhaps the most ironic thought is that we have no control over our thoughts!

That is what held Marsha captive and what made forgiving her brother seem impossible. As we talked, I challenged her to see that she was *not* at the mercy of the images haunting her like hideous ghosts. She was the landlord of her mind. She possessed exclusive power to welcome or evict any thought that wandered through the door. Our understanding of forgiveness must begin with this truth: By God's design, *you are the master of your mind*.

When Megapain Craters Your Life

Meteorites are particles of debris from the solar system that are heated by friction as they enter the earth's atmosphere before they impact the earth's surface. They can range in size from a grain of sand to a large boulder. Every day, as many as four billion meteorites fall to the earth, most of them miniscule in size.

Every day we are confronted with tests and trials, but on rare occasions, a severe crisis seems to come out of nowhere—a crisis so catastrophic it feels as if a massive meteorite has crashed down upon us. We can easily question the Master Creator, "Why would You allow this penetrating hurt? Why would You remove Your protective hand?" Usually our first response to megapain in our lives is to question God.

Faith can crumble and collapse under such intense pressure...or it can grow strong and secure when you choose to put your trust in God's plan. You need to know that He will use this traumatic trial for your good. And you need to rest that crushing meteorite before the throne of God, along with all your questions and megapain. Only then will you experience His megapeace; only then will you feel His mega-comfort.

This is not a foreign concept. We exercise mastery over our minds all the time. For example, we have a project with a deadline. As we look out the window, our thoughts drift off to la-la land. All of a sudden, we snap to attention and order our thoughts to fall back in line—much like soldiers in a military lineup.

Of course, after suffering a serious offense, our thoughts are much more intense than common daydreams, but the principle is still the same. *We are in charge of what we think.* That is why the apostle Paul tells us to "take *every thought captive* to make it obedient to Christ."[3] It *can* be done. You are the master of your mind!

How Can Mental Habits Trap You?

Marsha's story reveals certain warning signs that show how our negative thoughts can control us. Negative thoughts are a natural response to being wounded by someone. So often we are not even aware that our minds gravitate to negativity without any conscious decision. Noticing where our thoughts habitually take us is the first step toward gaining control over them.

You continually relive the offense

When we've been wounded by someone, we replay the event in our minds again and again...in slow motion and high definition. We are hypnotized by the scenes that cause us pain and we can't look away. We have a video loop playing the scenes over and over again.

We dwell on every detail; we inspect every stone of strife; we scrutinize every rock of cruelty; we even probe every pebble of apathy. No wonder we find it difficult to forgive when our wounds remain so fresh in our minds.

You imagine getting revenge

Sometimes we dwell on different scenarios based on what we *wish* had happened. *If only I had said...! If only I had done...!* Soon we begin to plot ways to get back at those who hurt us. The possibilities seem endless as we explore the dark pleasure in inventing how our revenge will unfold. Though we know we shouldn't, we imagine inflicting reciprocal pain on the offender.

> Revenge satisfies our longing for justice *temporarily,* but it leaves no room for healing *permanently.*

In essence, we picture ourselves eagerly reaching into our emotional bag, clasping our fingers around the most rugged rock we can find, and once retrieved, cocking our arm back for a vengeful hurl.

A team of psychologists who studied revenge reported their insights:

> Somewhere in the depths of our hearts, we get something out of nurturing fantasies of revenge. They keep us from being hurt again by the same person in the same way. They inspire anger, which makes us feel more powerful. They give us the mirage of raising our self-esteem because we are lowering the esteem in which we hold the other person.[4]

Revenge may satisfy our inner longing for justice *temporarily*, but it leaves no room for healing *permanently*.

You want bad things to befall your offender

Even when we don't go so far as to take personal revenge, we want our offender to suffer in other ways. (Maybe being pelted with rocks by somebody else!) Our unforgiving heart resents any success and delights in any failure experienced by our offender.

Because I so resented my father's success and so longed for some failure to humble him, imagine my astonishment when I read this scripture: "Do not gloat when your enemy falls; when he stumbles, do not let your heart rejoice."[5] No doubt this proverb condemned my own dark unforgiving thoughts.

Marsha wanted to forgive, but how could anything so heavy as her brother's offense be hoisted away? To dislodge so big a boulder from her mental bag felt impossible.

Convinced that her thoughts were immovable—even unavoidable—she felt powerless to stop her persistent mental images and replace them with thoughts that could pave the way to forgiveness. Like many people, she was ready to move on but lacked the practical tools that would help her take the first steps.

How Do We Retrain Our Brain to Forgive?

"If you have never *ever* prayed the Lord's Prayer—sometimes called 'the Model Prayer'—please raise your hand." I often issue this directive when teaching on forgiveness, and I have yet to see a single hand go up.

If you're among those who have ever prayed, "Forgive us our debts, as we also have forgiven our debtors,"[6] consider this: Did you really mean it? Think about it. If you really meant these words, then you are asking God to forgive you the exact same way you have forgiven those who have wronged you. Is that what you *really* want? If you're like everyone else, your first thought, in essence, is *God forbid!*

When we have been betrayed, the idea of giving the same grace given to us by God can seem beyond our grasp. Fortunately, we don't have to "get there" in one step or in one day. When a wound is deep, when an offense is great, when a boulder is big, *complete forgiveness* can only be a process. Danish author Isak Dinesen wrote, "When you have a great and difficult task, something perhaps almost impossible, if you only work a little at a time, every day a little, suddenly the work will finish itself."

Likewise, taking our every thought captive "to make it obedient to Christ" is not a short sprint, but a methodical marathon. The following seven strategies will help us win the race one step at a time.

1. *Acknowledge your thoughts, then give them to God.*

If a mugger attacks you, steals your money, and breaks your ribs, God wouldn't ask you to never think about it. That's impossible.

Equally impossible is to never think about an emotional rock that wounds you, steals your security, and breaks your heart.

When bruising boulders hit your heart, the key to success lies not in forgetting your thoughts, but in refusing to dwell on them. Over the years I have learned to acknowledge both the fact and the feeling—yes, a mugger mugged me and yes, I hurt. I then say, "Lord, I release the offense and the offender into Your hands." Sometimes I consciously stop and say, "This thought does not belong in my head but in Your hands. Here, Lord, it's Yours."

2. *Meditate on God's Word and speak it aloud.*

Sometimes those negative, nagging thoughts don't want to leave; therefore, this kind of "handoff" must be accompanied by positive comforting thoughts. Turning away unwanted thoughts is only the beginning—and not much good if we don't replace them with something else. A graphic illustration of the power of God's Word to literally destroy our rocks of resentment is found in Jeremiah 23:29, where the Lord Himself says, "Is not my word...like a hammer that breaks a rock in pieces?"

With that power available to us, we need not be defeated by destructive thoughts! What could be a better replacement than God's own thoughts, set down in His Word? Psalm 1:1-2 says, "Blessed is the man who does not walk in the counsel of the wicked or stand in the way of sinners or sit in the seat of mockers. But his delight is in the law of the LORD, and on his law he meditates day and night." Meditating on God's Word is a powerful way to fill in those destructive ruts and chart a new path leading to forgiveness.

When Marsha would fall into the habit of mentally reliving the crimes against her daughter, she felt vulnerable, alone, and defenseless. Although she needed to acknowledge these thoughts and give them to God, she also needed to *replace them* with a vision of God's power and protective care. To do so, she needed to reach for her Bible and begin absorbing the truths of God. Most people are unaware of the power of God's Word to be a major part of healing. God hasn't put this truth under a rock, hiding it from us. Psalm 107:20 proclaims, "He sent forth His *word* and *healed* them."

Bottom line: God's Word heals the hurts in our hearts!

For years I've been drawn to one short verse found in the longest psalm, which is the longest chapter in the Bible. Psalm 119:50 reads, "My comfort in my suffering is this: Your promise preserves my life!"

Again, God's Word heals our hearts!

Marsha could read these words out loud, and feel the peace of God begin to soothe her wounds. Because timeworn habits refuse to leave quickly, Marsha must refuse her harmful thoughts and replace them with God's healing thoughts—not just once, but purposely repeating the counsel of God's Word over

> By thanking and praising God, you replace the negative with the positive.

and over. With such repetition, Marsha will realize that her emotional bag of bitterness has become lighter.

3. *Use your power tools: thanksgiving and praise.*

In his book *Our Heavenly Father*, Dr. Robert Frost writes, "There is nothing more precious to God than our praise during affliction.... What he does not protect us from, he will perfect us through. There is indeed a special blessing for those who do not become offended at God during adversity."[7]

What can protect you from becoming offended at God for what He allows in your life? Every day you swim in an ocean filled with the gifts of God—these are the blessings of God. Start a new habit of beginning your mornings by expressing gratitude for your many gifts from God: your ability to think, to move, to feel, etc. Or thank Him for certain people you love or certain situations you appreciate.

By thanking God and praising Him, you replace negative with the positive. With pad and pen in hand, do this project: The first morning list five gifts, the second morning add four other gifts to your list, the third morning add three, the fourth morning add two, and then add one gift every day for as long as you feel the need. Thank God for each gift and continue adding to your list each day for a minimum of one month. This prayer project is a powerful way to keep control of your thoughts.[8]

Whenever a scripture is repeated in the Bible, that verse is highly significant. If the passage is again mentioned a third time, that verse has *huge* significance. Such is the repetition of this verse in the Psalms, "Why are you downcast, O my soul? Why so disturbed within me? Put your hope in God, for I will yet praise him, my Savior and my God."[9] Even when your heart is downcast, praise God that He still is your Savior.

It is impossible to perpetually think of yourself as a victim when you make a practice of thanking God for specific blessings in your life. Stacking blessing upon blessing breaks down the layers of resentment that can build up in your mind.

It is also impossible to dwell on "an eye for an eye" justice (otherwise called revenge) while giving praise to God for His infinite love and mercy. In setting your thoughts on thanksgiving and praise, you remind yourself of how much you have been given—and forgiven. You will feel energized as you think of getting rid of all that rancorous rubble in your emotional bag.

4. *Pray for your enemies.*

Never will I forget a woman who had just prayed to receive Jesus as her Lord and Savior—a divorced woman whose husband had continually violated their marriage. Because her pain was still fresh, I suggested she pray for him to see his need for the Savior to pray for his salvation.

Startled, she protested, "Oh no—I don't want him in heaven with me!"

Now *I* was startled. I prayed, *Help me, Lord*. I paused, then posed, "But he wouldn't be the same man." She looked puzzled. "If he genuinely received Jesus as his Lord and Savior—and gave Christ control of his life—he wouldn't be the same man. He would have to change." Slowly she began to nod her head. So I continued, "The Bible says, 'If anyone is in Christ, he is a new creation; old things have passed away; behold, all things have become new.'[10] As an authentic Christian, Christ would live inside him. Therefore, he would *have* to change. He would no longer have his old sinful nature; instead, he would have Christ's nature inside him."

"Oh, I see!" she exclaimed. "Then I will definitely pray for him."

When struggling to pray for those who persecute you, realize that your enemies are not spiritually healthy, or else they would not have hurt you. They too are wounded. They too are dragging around heavy bags of emotional hurts and are in need of God's healing.

Praying for others helps us to see them as God sees them. It paves the way to forgive as God forgives. Praying for your enemies enables you to more easily take them off of your hook and place them onto God's hook.

5. *Practice forgiving the daily wrongs.*

When you struggle to forgive someone for a boulder size offense, ask yourself, How do I handle small offenses—those pebble-sized hurts that slip insidiously into the bottom of my emotional bag? Our daily lives are filled with routine affronts: A family member who is too flippant, a co-worker who cuts in line, a finicky friend, an abrasive boss, an annoying neighbor, a rude stranger.

Mundane offenses are opportunities to forgive, just as surely as major ones. If we don't forgive the small stuff, it's unlikely we will forgive the big stuff. Conversely, if we don't forgive the big stuff, it's unlikely we will forgive the small stuff.

God's forgiveness covers every offense, no matter the size. Why?

Because His forgiveness has nothing to do with the offense, but everything to do with *Him*. Just as God loves because He is a loving God, He forgives because He is a forgiving God.

When Jesus taught us to pray, "Forgive us our debts, as we also have forgiven our debtors,"[11] He meant it to be a *daily* prayer. He meant forgiveness to be your *way of life*—just as it is His—and not just reserved for extraordinary times. That means turning your burlap bags inside out and shaking them until every last boulder, rock, stone, pebble, and all their gravelly remains are gone.

But that's not all. To be totally free—to forever enjoy the freedom of forgiveness—there's one more thing you need to do: *Cut the bottom out of your bag*. That will prevent any rock, stone, or pebble from being able to be collected in the first place.

6. *Surround yourself with supportive people who tell you the truth.*

When we have been wounded, we naturally seek out people who can help apply the salve of support and sympathy. So far, so good. But that salve of sympathy can too easily turn into further inflammation of the wound. The medicine of a listening ear, meant to speed healing, can turn into rehashing of painful events and bashing of our offenders. Such so-called "medicine" only keeps the wound fresh.

If you catch yourself reaching for the phone to call someone who would keep open the wound of unforgiveness, *stop!* Instead, dial a friend who may wound you for the moment by not telling you what you want to hear, but who will also encourage you to forgive so your heart can be healed. The book of Proverbs speaks of this kind of friend: "Faithful are the wounds of a friend."[12]

What we need are friends who help us rethink our thoughts—friends who challenge us to not stay in the rut of unforgiveness, friends who will counsel us to forgive even when we don't feel like it.

7. *Turn thought into action.*

The apostle James posed this question: "What good is it...if a man claims to have faith but has no deeds? Can such faith save him?"[13] We can also ask, What good is forgiveness if it produces no evidence? You can easily *say* you have forgiven someone, but the proof comes in what you are willing to *do* about it. Once you "retrain your brain" by choosing to forgive—even when you don't feel like it—you can "seal" your choice by giving the offender a gift. Counselor Robert Enright explains:

> This point in the forgiveness process may surprise some. Why should we give the offender a gift? We are, after all, the injured party. The offender owes us, we don't owe anything. But by giving a gift to the one who has hurt us, we break the power that person has over us.[14]

You might be thinking, *What? You want me to give a gift to the guilty? To forgive a debt is one matter, to give a gift is another!* Yet this is precisely what Jesus says to us: "If someone wants to sue you and take your [shirt], let him have your [coat] as well. If someone forces you to go one mile, go with him two miles."[15]

The purpose of giving both your shirt and your coat—the purpose of going a second mile beyond the first—is not to *reward* the guilty. Not at all. It is so that you will adopt the heart and mind of Jesus. The purpose for all of us is to allow a forgiving God to turn us into a forgiving people.

≈

Forgiveness as a Way of Life

A year passed before I heard from Marsha again. Numerous times I thought about her severe anguish and vexation over her own brother sexually abusing her precious daughter. But now I couldn't help but notice a distinct difference in her voice.

"I've come a long way since we last spoke. I appreciated how you helped me replace my destructive thoughts with constructive ones, even though I thought it was impossible. It wasn't easy, but it wasn't impossible, either."

I asked how she was feeling emotionally.

"I still experience moments of pain—perhaps I always will. But my feelings no longer dominate my life. Every time I think about the abuse, I choose to forgive my brother. I'm no longer a prisoner of my emotions."

As Marsha discovered, forgiveness is not a one-time event. It is a way of life. Every memory of abuse had been another boulder of bitterness inside her soul. But when she began to take charge of her mind and chose a new way of thinking, she cut the bottom out of the bag.

You too can cut the bottom out of your bag. As Marsha said, it isn't easy, but it isn't impossible, either.

8

ROCKS AREN'T
REMOVED OVERNIGHT

The Four Stages of Forgiveness

BETH COULDN'T UNDERSTAND WHY bitterness and anger kept bubbling up like molten lava spewing from a dormant volcano. After all, she had forgiven her husband and the woman—the former "friend"—who had betrayed her and so deeply wounded her.

At least Beth *thought* she had forgiven them.

The details of the drama were all too common. In fact, Beth later said, "The whole thing seemed like a pitiful, predictable plot from a cheesy novel. The unsuspecting wife is always the last to know! How could I have not seen it?"

What she hadn't seen was the affair her husband, Derek, and her best friend, Carrie, had begun several years before. Their secret came to light when one of Beth's co-workers spotted them dining together at a fancy restaurant in an adjacent town. At first, Beth refused to believe her husband would cheat on her so blatantly. He was a leader in their church and a respected member of the community.

But more and more clues began to accumulate, confirming for Beth the truth of their conspiracy: hushed phone calls, mysterious expenses, unplanned trips, and late business meetings.

When Beth confronted Derek, he denied the affair, weaving elaborate fabrications to cover his tracks. But eventually, as Beth presented airtight evidence, he could do nothing but admit the truth. Devastated, Beth immediately issued an ultimatum: End the affair, or end the marriage! She set firm boundaries with Derek, insisting on marriage counseling for as long as she felt it was necessary.

Beth also confronted Carrie, who only offered lame excuses and rationalizations: "We never intended for it to happen...we weren't looking to get involved...we just fell into it...we never meant to hurt you."

All of this inflamed Beth because Carrie, her confidant, had become "the other woman." Beth had confided in her closest friend many times—this was the person with whom she had spent countless hours laughing, dreaming, and planning.

Beth felt her heart continually being crushed by too heavy a boulder.

To work through her grief and anger, Beth joined a support group. The other members listened patiently as Beth vented and poured

Setting Stones in the Cobblestone

Cobblestones are smooth, round rocks typically picked from riverbeds to create pavement for streets and sidewalks. While *cobbled* refers to something *roughly assembled*, the very *imprecise setting* of the rocks create the charm of a cobblestone street.

For the times you've felt forgotten, overlooked, or unnoticed, the pain of rejection runs deep. Realize that rejection is one step away from resentment. And resentment is merely the result of an unforgiving heart.

You may feel like a "throwaway"—like a useless stone thoughtlessly hurled into the water, like a forgotten stone on the riverbed of life. But God has not forgotten you.

Whenever you feel the pain of unforgiveness, give those stones of hostility—those stones of scorn—to the Master Paver. Amazing benefits await you. When in His hands, He knows what to do with them and where to put them. He puts them in the right places on His path...so that each and every painful experience has eternal purpose.

out her heart over the course of several months. A few tried to solve Beth's problems and speed along the healing.

"You've just got to leave all that behind," one woman said. "It's time to let go and move on."

"You know God wants total restoration for you and Derek," another said. "Derek asked forgiveness, and now it's up to you to grant it."

One person painted a word picture about placing all of her heart-aches in a metal box, locking it tight, and tossing it into the depths of the ocean. There, it would stay forever—never to wash up on the shore of her life again.

Beth knew these people meant well. But their advice made her only feel worse. She felt guilty that she couldn't completely forgive. She felt like a second-rate Christian for not being able to access the healing power of God as others said she must.

She felt ashamed at the times when her venomous rage returned. She felt herself limping her way through life as if she had giant "stone bruises" on the bottoms of her feet. Walking was excruciatingly painful; running in the freedom of forgiveness seemed utterly impossible.

On the road to healing and forgiveness, Beth had run into an insurmountable stone wall—or so she thought.

This was about the time Beth called our radio program, *Hope in the Night,* and shared her story. Her voice quivered, "It's been almost two years since my husband ended his affair. We went through a year of counseling. We met with our pastor for several months. Derek has been in an accountability group, and I joined a support group. I believe he is genuinely contrite—in fact, he's deeply remorseful about what he did. But…"

Beth's voice trailed off. I prompted her to continue. "But things are not neat and tidy, are they?" I asked. "You think you should be over it by now, but it's not that easy, is it?"

"No, and I don't understand. I've forgiven Derek. I really have. I've even forgiven Carrie. But sometimes I still feel overwhelming anger, and I know that isn't right. Many times I've uttered words of forgiveness, but my emotions don't seem to be listening."

During those kinds of calls, I want to reach across the airwaves and put my arms around those who are hurting. But I can't, so I offer comfort by explaining God's grace as best I can. Beth's emotions were leading her into despair, and she needed peace and hope. What I told Beth is what I want to tell everyone who struggles with the

> Forgiveness is a gift you give yourself—the gift of a heart at peace.

residue of resentment—with the wounds of the past that won't seem to heal: "When the offense is severe, forgiveness does not happen easily. Real forgiveness is a slow, difficult, painful process."

Boulders can't just be tossed aside as if they were tiny pebbles.

"Forgiveness is ultimately *freeing*, but typically not *fast*. That may not come as good news, because we would like our pain and turmoil to quickly disappear. But the pain and anguish you're experiencing is perfectly normal, even healthy. When people take shortcuts through the forgiveness process, they are merely putting Band-Aids on deep wounds. It doesn't work, and real healing never happens." Deep wounds must heal from the inside out.

This is precisely the danger of using the biblical admonition, "Do not let the sun go down while you are still angry"[1] as a holy hammer to rebuke anyone who fails to totally dispense with anger before a literal sundown. Certainly, we can't expect anger to dissipate if we nurse it and rehearse it from one day to the next. However, once we examine the root cause of our swelling angst and replace harmful thoughts with healing thoughts, then we satisfy the spirit of this teaching.

Why Don't Quick Fixes Work?

In 1969, physician Dr. Elisabeth Kubler-Ross introduced to the world the stages of grieving in her landmark book *On Death and*

Dying. This revolutionary work helped millions of people identify, understand, and deal with the process associated with the end-of-life experience. When a patient is diagnosed with a terminal illness, typically the mental and emotional reaction consists of five stages: denial, anger, bargaining for time, depression, and acceptance.

I can't help thinking about these stages whenever I broach the subject of forgiveness. That's because the process of forgiveness must follow distinct stages in order to bring about true resolution.

Notice I've used the word *process* several times. Forgiveness involves a progression, a series of decisions with actions that build on each other. This is why many people get stuck in their resentment—they want to quickly forgive and move on. But complete healing comes gradually and incrementally.

We have to reach to reach deep into our emotional bag of hurts and painstakingly dislodge the rocks of resentment that have become wedged tightly together and refuse to budge.

For most people, that's difficult to accept, because we live in an "instant" society. Being accustomed to quick and easy solutions, we expect everything to happen immediately. We want it now.

For you to empty every stone of hostility from your emotional bag requires your commitment to *continuously* cleanse your soul and spirit.

Many like Beth cling to the misconception that forgiving someone is a once-and-for-all decision. They buy into the pervasive clichés "Forgive and forget," "Let go and let God," or worse yet, "Get over it!" as if that's the end of it.

What Are the Four Stages of Forgiveness?

Because forgiveness is often difficult to give, you will find it helpful to work through a four-stage process. And as you do, keep in mind that forgiveness is a gift you ultimately give yourself—the gift of a joyful heart. It is grudge-free living. It is true freedom. It is the rich, rewarding life God wants you to experience.

God wants to rid you of poisonous bitterness—like the deadly poison Captain Meriwether Lewis was exposed to during the Lewis and Clark expedition.

According to a journal entry dated August 22, 1804, these two famous explorers arrived at a bluff that displayed numerous types of rocks—valuable rocks containing alum, copperas, cobalt, and pyrites. While testing the quality of the minerals, Lewis tasted the cobalt and breathed its fumes, and was almost poisoned to death. As a remedy for the bitter poison, Lewis took a dose of salts to alleviate its deadly effect.[2]

There is a remedy for the poisonous rocks of resentment in our lives. This healing remedy involves the four stages of forgiveness—stages that banish bitterness with all its toxic effects—once and for all.

Someone once said, "Freedom is what you do with what's been

Toxic Unforgiveness

Cobalt, found in various ores, can become a lustrous hard metal with many applications. Its compounds are used in a variety of paints and ink, but its most beautiful application is the pigment of cobalt blue for coloring enamel, glass, tile, and porcelain. Cobalt is also a necessary element for human life—a small amount is part of vitamin B12—but too much in your system can be toxic to the lungs and heart.

Unforgiveness, too, can poison your heart and even contaminate your spirit. Any poison in the heart can be just as emotionally and spiritually fatal as allowing too much cobalt inside your body.

Rather than allowing the venom of vindictiveness to harm you, you can allow the Master Physician to bring a healing you could never imagine...and a hope you couldn't have on your own. When you give your poisonous rocks to Him, He will heal you with His extraordinary love. He will free you to have His extraordinary forgiveness, and your toxic unforgiveness will be gone!

done to you." I couldn't agree more. The greatest payoff for working through the stages of forgiveness is the new freedom you gain to expel bitterness, to enjoy relationships, and to experience wholeness, just as God intends.

Stage One: *Face the Offense*

The first step is often the hardest: accurately see the offense for what it is. Before extending complete forgiveness, you must acknowledge the gravity of the offense and the magnitude of the problem—plus the pain it created. You have to face the truth and sift through all the resulting heartaches. Many become stuck at this stage because offenses are frustrating at best and infuriating at worst.

There's not a person on earth who wouldn't prefer to avoid facing pain. And, sadly, most people do. I say sadly because *experiencing pain is the conduit to healing*. But healing begins with facing the truth—with facing the fact that you have rocks of pain in your emotional bag.

Jesus says to His followers, "You will know the truth, and the truth will set you free."[3] There's nothing in this statement to suggest knowing truth and experiencing freedom occurs rapidly and painlessly. I recall the fascinating title of an old book, *The Truth Will Set You Free, But First It Will Make You Miserable*. How true.

Some say, "As soon as that horrendous ordeal happened, I forgave him. That's what I've been taught to do." In fact, a lot of well-intentioned people feel guilty if they don't extend immediate, complete forgiveness. They try to forgive without confronting the depth and breadth of the offense and grieving over it. Rarely is the full impact of mistreatment felt at the moment it occurs. Rather, its aftermath is experienced at different levels over a period of time. Therefore, forgiveness needs to be extended again and again at each different level of impact.

I frequently talk with those who hinder true healing by rationalizing the offense: "No matter how badly he treats me, he doesn't mean any harm by it." And some are bent on minimizing the offense: "Worse things have happened to other people." But the truth is that *no amount of harmful behavior is acceptable.* There is no excuse for bad treatment of any kind—anytime, anywhere, anyway. As the apostle Paul says, "Have nothing to do with the fruitless deeds of darkness, but rather expose them."[4]

Others fail to face the truth by excusing the offender's conduct: "He just didn't realize what he was doing." Or, "I shouldn't feel upset with him. He's a member of my family." No matter the age of the offender, and no matter our relationship to the offender, an offense is an offense, a wrong is a wrong. We need to recognize injustice for what it is and we need to call sin *sin*. We must face the truth instead of trying to dismiss or excuse it. The writer of Proverbs said, "Whoever says to the guilty, 'You are innocent'—people will curse him."[5]

Stage Two: *Feel the Offense*

In response to unjust treatment, we may feel anger, outrage, or even hatred. Still, some people avoid dealing honestly with their emotions because they believe it's inappropriate or un-Christian to hate. But not all hatred is wrong. God hates evil. The Bible says, "There is a time for everything, and a season for every activity under heaven...a time to love and a time to hate."[6] All our rock-hard emotions need to be excavated rather than allowed to stay buried. Failing to acknowledge and experience pain results in rigid responses: suppression of feelings or outright denial.

Some people insist, "Her gossiping about me doesn't really hurt—even though we are the best of friends. It was probably just a slip of the tongue, and who hasn't been guilty of that?" The truth is, being mistreated by someone you love *is* painful, and *does* bother you. Without *feeling*, there can be no *healing*.

Notice how frequently the Bible mentions raw emotions. The psalmist wrote, "Out of the depths, I cry to you, O LORD."[7] And the prophet Jeremiah cried out, "Why is my pain unending and my wound grievous and incurable?"[8] Such gut-level outpouring is therapeutic and curative.

However, when feelings are neglected or ignored, they become landmines in a war zone, buried beneath the surface, dangerous and explosive. The only way to eliminate their potential threat is to defuse them or detonate them. In either case, like landmines, they must be identified and handled with great care.

Stage Three: *Forgive the Offender*

Perhaps you know the famous words, "To err is human, to forgive divine."[9] In the living room of my home, I have a small, blue and white Delft tile that always makes me smile. It reads, "To err is human, to blame it on somebody else is more human!" That is so true! How much easier it is to nurture resentment than deal with forgiveness. But we are called by God to both seek forgiveness and extend it. And when we do extend it, our lives take on the divine character of Christ.

Once you have worked through the first two stages— you've faced the offense and felt

> Forgiveness is not a feeling, but rather an act of the will— a decision we make.

the offense—you've laid the groundwork for true forgiveness to take place. Still, many people conceive all kinds of arguments to avoid taking this next step. See if any of these sound familiar:

Argument: "I shouldn't forgive when I don't feel like forgiving. It wouldn't be genuine."

Response: As we've already noted, forgiveness is not a feeling, but rather an act of the will—a decision we make. Jesus affirmed this by saying, "When you stand praying, if you hold anything against anyone, forgive him, so that your Father in heaven may forgive you your sins."[10] He didn't say, "Wait for loving feelings to kick in and *then* forgive." Surely Jesus knew that if we all waited until we *feel* like forgiving, few of us would ever get around to it.

Argument: "I can forgive everyone else, but God knows I don't have the power to forgive one particular person."

Response: The issue is not your lack of power to forgive, but rather how strong God's power is within you. As Peter wrote, "His divine power has given us everything we need for life and godliness through our knowledge of him who called us by his own glory and goodness."[11]

Argument: "Forgiveness doesn't seem fair. She ought to pay for her wrong! She can't get off scot-free!"

Response: God knows how to deal with each person fairly, and He will, in His own time and His own way. When we try to determine what punishment should be doled out for someone who wronged us, we assume a role that isn't rightly ours. As the apostle Paul said, "Do not take revenge, my friends, but leave room for God's wrath, for it is written: 'It is mine to avenge; I will repay,' says the Lord."[12]

Argument: "I have forgiven, but it doesn't do any good. He keeps doing the same thing over and over."

Response: You cannot control what others do, but you can control *how you respond* to what others do. Jesus said you are to respond with forgiveness no matter the number of times wronged.[13] Understand that the willingness to forgive—repeatedly, if necessary—does not mean we allow ourselves to be trampled upon like a doormat. There is nothing noble or godly about remaining passive in the face of persistent mistreatment that can be avoided.

Argument: "I cannot forgive and forget. I keep thinking about being hurt."

Response: When you choose to forgive, you don't get a case of "holy amnesia." However, you can close off your mind to rehearsing the pain of the past. Choose not to replay the hurtful event over and over. Refuse to bring up the offense again. Paul wrote,

"Forgetting what is behind and straining toward what is ahead, I press on toward the goal to win the prize for which God has called me heavenward in Christ Jesus."[14] I'm glad he used the phrases "straining toward" and "press on" because they imply the *effort* required to leave behind not only the things we formerly gloried in, but also past hurts and failings.

Stage Four: *Find Oneness*

Author and physician Richard Swenson said,

> Broken relationships are a razor across the artery of the spirit. Stemming the hemorrhage and binding the wound should be done as quickly as possible. Yet all too often it takes months or years. And sometimes the bleeding never stops…. It is not revenge that heals. It is not litigation, or time, or distance that heals. It is forgiveness and—when possible—reconciliation that bring wholeness. True reconciliation is one of the most powerful of all human interactions. This is not a matter of human psychology but rather a divine gift.[15]

Relationships filled with resentment ultimately perish; relationships filled with forgiveness ultimately prevail. However, the restoration of oneness is contingent on several factors. When these conditions are met and both parties are committed to reconciliation, then the two can be of one mind and one heart. The Bible says, "If you have any encouragement from being united with Christ, if any comfort from his love, if any fellowship with the Spirit, if any tenderness and compassion, then make my joy complete by being like-minded, having the same love, being one in spirit and purpose."[16]

What Are the Prerequisites for Restored Relationships?

A damaged relationship can be restored when both parties are committed to honesty in the relationship. I use the acronym H-O-N-E-S-T-Y to demonstrate the elements involved in this process:

Honestly evaluate yourself and your relationship. God intends to use your relationship to reveal your weaknesses and to strengthen your relationship with Him. Evaluate your own weaknesses and the weaknesses within your relationship so you can know where change needs to take place.[17]

Open your heart and share your pain. Have a candid conversation with your offender. Fully explain the pain you have suffered and the sorrow in your heart. Don't attack, and don't heap on guilt. Instead, address the offense and explain how it made you feel.[18]

Notice whether your offender takes responsibility. The person who wronged you needs to know that the offending incident struck like an arrow into your heart. Offenders who ignore your pain and refuse to be accountable are not ready for reconciliation because they are not ready to take responsibility. They must acknowledge your pain and demonstrate godly sorrow.[19]

Expect your offender to be completely truthful. Promises need to be made and safeguards established regarding honesty, support, and loyalty within the relationship. Although you cannot guarantee someone else's dependability, you should be able to discern whether there is sincerity and truthfulness.[20]

Set appropriate boundaries for the relationship. Has the other person crossed the line regarding what is appropriate (excessively angry, possessive, demeaning, insensitive, irresponsible, prideful, abusive)? If so, explain what the boundary line is, what the repercussion is for a boundary violation (a limited relationship), and what the reward is for respecting the boundary (increased trust). You need to be disciplined enough to hold your offender accountable, and your offender needs to become disciplined enough to stop undermining the relationship.[21]

Take time, cautiously think, and sincerely pray before you let your offender all the way back into your heart. When trust has been trampled, integrity and consistency are needed to prove that your offender is now trustworthy. Change takes time. Therefore, don't rush the relationship. Confidence is not regained overnight—and trust is not given, but earned.[22]

Yield your heart to starting over. God wants you to have a heart that is yielded to His perfect will for your life. Serious offenses will reshape your future, and you will not be able to come back together with your offender as though nothing ever happened. You personally change through pain. You take on new roles, and you cannot simply abandon your new places in life the moment a friend is forgiven and is invited back into your heart and life.

> When you forgive, you are no longer bound by what *has been* but by what *can be*.

Once you begin to cut the ties that bind you to past hurts and heartaches, each day becomes an opportunity for positive choices. You are no longer bound by what *has been* but by what *can be*. You can now determine the direction of your life and are no longer leaving it to the ghosts of your past.[23]

Set Free from Anger: Rob's Story

"I want a divorce." Those were the last words "Rob" expected to hear after returning home from a three-day Promise Keepers conference. But that evening, his wife "Rita" was unusually quiet and remote. When he asked her why, her anguish poured out in a flood of emotions. She explained that during the days he was gone, a new sense of peace and calm had settled over their household.

"During the past three days, I've felt better about myself than I've ever felt during our marriage. In fact, I've felt a hundred times better about who I am. Why? Because you weren't here. Because I didn't have to worry constantly about your next temper tantrum, your next outburst, or your next put-down." She swallowed hard and told him she wanted out of the marriage.

For Rob, this painful moment of truth cut deeply.

Rita agreed to attend counseling as a last-ditch effort to save their marriage. After a few sessions, the counselor identified the rock-bottom issue: Rob had a problem with unresolved anger, which fueled his periodic rages.

Failing to address significant past hurts turned his emotions into a boiling, churning cauldron, agitating all those rocks, stones, and boulders in his ready-to-burst bag. It didn't take much to make his inner "toxic waste" spew out like a steaming geyser and injure anyone who happened to be within range. Most often that was Rita, who was left wounded, hurt, and frightened.

What was his reaction when the counselor brought all this to light?

"I got mad at him!" Rob recalled. "At one point, I yelled and stormed out of the room." The counselor's observations pricked Rob's spirit—the thought that *he* needed to change was too much to withstand.

Several months later, unable to resolve their differences, Rob and Rita divorced. But by the grace of God, Rob's journey of healing was just about to begin.

One sleepless night, a few months after his marriage fell apart, Rob turned on the radio. *Hope in the Night* was airing the topic of anger. He listened intently and then ordered our set of resources on anger. With those in hand, he reserved a hotel room for an intense weekend of reading, listening, and praying in order to grasp God's principles for overcoming unresolved anger. It wasn't long before Rob recognized the severity of his problem.

"It hit me like a ton of bricks. I frequently reacted to people—especially Rita—with rage. I'd get so angry that I'd become irrational and out of control."

One night, Rob penned this journal entry: "I look back upon my countless explosive episodes with regret and remorse. It grieves me deeply to realize how I damaged so many people—my ex-wife, my son, my mother, my employees. However, Christ is healing me as I understand the source of my anger—and He is healing my relationships as I seek forgiveness from those I harmed."

Rob's progress and healing took considerable time as month after month he gained insight upon insight into how his past was affecting his present.

"God gradually revealed the source of my anger—profound hurt and rejection from my childhood and teenage years. When I raged at my wife, I'd been trying to control her so she couldn't reject me. But in reality, I was only making things worse." When Rob couldn't control his wife, he became out of control.

When Rob forgave those who had wounded him in the past, he was set free from the anger that was destroying his present relationships and jeopardizing his future ones. Today, Rob reports that he has a good relationship with Rita, who has since remarried. In fact, he recently received a letter from her, thanking him for his compassionate and Christlike attitude in the years following their divorce.

"I'm a work in progress," he said humbly. "I still get angry sometimes, but now I'm able to step back and understand why. I understand better the source of my once-overpowering emotions. Best of all, I know how to express my feelings constructively."

Rob had been a prisoner of his own unmanageable anger. For many years, he was shackled to a heavy bag of emotional hurts which was the impetus for him to act and react in cruel ways. But through God's guidance and healing—and his own courage to confront the truth—Rob was unshackled from the anger that controlled his life. He had given Christ control of his life, and he was now set free.

As the psalmist wrote, "The LORD sets prisoners free, the LORD gives sight to the blind, the LORD lifts up those who are bowed down, the LORD loves the righteous."[24] Like Rob, all of us can be boulder-free, bag-free, shackle-free!

STEERING CLEAR OF STONE THROWERS

*Forgiveness Is One Thing,
Reconciliation Is Another*

"I KNEW VICKY LED a wild life when she was younger," Clint told me on *Hope in the Night*. "She was open about all the bad things she'd done and poor choices she'd made. But I believed all that was behind her. I thought her 'rebellious streak' had ended years ago. I guess it was just lurking in the shadows, waiting to re-emerge."

Vicky, his wife of eight years, turned his life upside down when she left him and their two children to live with an old boyfriend she had dated before becoming a Christian. Upon moving out, she got a job serving drinks in a local bar. Not long after that she was arrested for drunk driving and possession of marijuana. It was as if she had become a different person overnight, shattering their marriage into pieces.

"It just came out of nowhere. I was totally devastated."

By the time Clint called me, he had done the hard work of beginning to forgive Vicky. In spite of his struggles with the deep pain of betrayal, Clint understood that forgiveness does not depend on emotions. Sure, he grappled with anger and the natural impulse to retaliate in some way. Certainly, he had times when he felt like pulling rocks of rage from his burlap bag and hurling them at her. But over time, he made great progress in steering his thoughts away from revenge and fixing them on God's Word. Every day he felt the burden of unforgiveness grow lighter as he slowly let go of Vicky's betrayal.

So why did Clint now feel the need to call me? Because Vicky had finally asked for the forgiveness he had been learning to extend to her.

"She came to see me last night. She was crying. She said she made the biggest mistake of her life and she's sorry."

"That's good. That's the beginning of repentance. I imagine she's got a long way to go, but admitting her mistakes is the place to start."

"That's true, but..." Clint hesitated, and I immediately understood his problem.

"Did she ask to come back home?"

"Yes, she did, and I just don't know what to do. I feel so guilty. She said she wants to start over and be a family again. I suppose that's possible, but I don't trust her anymore. Is that wrong? I believe I've genuinely forgiven her, but I have serious doubts about trying to pick up where we left off. When God said to forgive, does that mean we have to be reconciled, too?"

That question said it all. Clint had worked through the need to extend unconditional forgiveness, but he was not prepared for the thorny issue of reconciliation. It's thorny because many people don't know there is a difference between forgiving someone and restoring a relationship with someone—between keeping your bag empty by removing rocks and by avoiding rocks! In fact, a lot of people resist forgiving others altogether because of this thorny issue. They fear that forgiving a person requires re-establishing a relationship with that person. They say, "If I forgive someone who has hurt me, I'll look weak and spineless and give the impression that it's okay to hurt me."

The truth is, forgiving someone *and* holding firm boundaries go hand in hand. Forgiveness must include built-in protections that prevent further mistreatment.

Clint called because he was afraid forgiving Vicky meant

All That Glitters...

Pyrite is a sulfide mineral with isometric crystals that appear in cubic form. Its brassy yellow hue and metallic luster have fostered the nickname *fool's gold*. Though pyrite looks like the real thing, it's not—proving that not everything that glitters is gold.

The words *I'm sorry* or *I forgive you* can't always be trusted either. When genuinely expressed, they can be a powerful impetus toward reconciliation. But when they ring hollow with false forgiveness, the words are "just words"... which makes them just as deceptive as fool's gold. A begrudging, halfhearted admission of guilt does nothing to rebuild trust—and trust is paramount to achieving a reconciled relationship.

When you give your pieces of broken pyrite to God—the hollow apologies and insincere sorrys—the Master Refiner transforms them into 24-carat gold...into purest gold within your soul. And your transformation is not dependent on what anyone else does or doesn't do—only on what the Refiner does with you as you yield your will to His. Through His refining process, you become real, authentic, and genuine...for with God, "All that glitters is purest gold."

automatically renewing their relationship as husband and wife. He had no reason to trust her to not bring her resurgent drug and alcohol problems with her, and he knew they couldn't rebuild their marriage on a bedrock of bedlam.

However, Clint wanted to obey God. He was desperate to know what God expected of him—whether he should reconcile with Vicky, despite potential harm to himself and their children. I assured him that God did not expect him to put his family in harm's way.

Forgiveness vs. Reconciliation: What's the Difference?

Don't get me wrong—reconciliation after an offense is wonderful. In fact, reconciliation is the ideal. It's the goal to strive for.

Still, forgiveness and reconciliation are not the same. In fact, their differences are many:

- *Forgiveness* can take place with only one person; *reconciliation* requires the involvement of at least two persons.

- *Forgiveness* is directed one way; *reconciliation* is reciprocal, occurring two ways.

- *Forgiveness* is a decision to release the person who harmed you; *reconciliation* is the effort to rejoin the person who harmed you.

- *Forgiveness* involves a change in thinking *about* the offender; *reconciliation* involves a change in behavior *by* the offender.

- *Forgiveness* is a free gift to the one who has broken trust; *reconciliation* is a restored relationship based on restored trust.

- *Forgiveness* is extended even if it is never earned; *reconciliation* is offered to the offender because it has been earned.

- *Forgiveness* is unconditional regardless of a lack of repentance; *reconciliation* is conditional based on repentance.

The bottom line is that reconciliation, unlike forgiveness, is a *joint venture*. It takes two committed people to repair and re-establish a damaged relationship. Reconciliation focuses on the relationship, whereas forgiveness requires no relationship. Both sides must reach out if reconciliation is going to work.

> God always wants peace *with* us and *between* us.

With forgiveness, the forgiver must take a giant step forward regardless of what the offender does. With reconciliation, the offender *and* the forgiver take a giant step toward each other. Both parties must invest equally in the outcome. This means reconciliation requires a relationship in which two people are willing to walk together toward the same goal. As the Bible says, "Do two walk together unless they have agreed to do so?"[1]

The Road to Reconciliation: The Prodigal Son's Story

In the familiar parable of the prodigal son, we know the father forgave long before his son repented and came home. In doing so, he saved himself the torment of constant bitterness. He was free to get on with his life. But that's not where the story ends. The father's deepest longing was to have his son back again. He watched and waited for that chance, and seized it when it came.

God always wants peace *with* us and *between* us. He paid a high price for reconciliation with the world, and then passed that ministry on to us. The Bible says that God

> reconciled us to himself through Christ and *gave us the ministry of reconciliation:* that God was reconciling the world to himself in Christ, not counting men's sins against them. And he has committed to us the message of reconciliation. We are therefore Christ's ambassadors, as though God were making his appeal through us. We implore you on Christ's behalf: Be reconciled to God.[2]

Does that mean we have failed if our forgiveness does not always lead to reconciliation? Since we are to forgive no matter what, must we also reconcile no matter what? The answer is no!

Returning home, the repentant prodigal said, "Father, I have sinned against heaven and against you. I am no longer worthy to be called your son."[3] The father immediately restored his son to his former place in the family, and threw a party to celebrate his son's return.

Suppose the son had said, "Hey, old man, I ran out of money. Give me some more and I'll be outta here faster than you can say 'wine, women, and song.' "

In this case, the story would have ended without reconciliation. The father extending forgiveness and wanting oneness would still not be enough to bring about reconciliation.

How Does Trust Affect Reconciliation?

The essential element in reconciliation is *restored trust*. Surely Aristotle was talking about trust when he said, "Wishing to be friends is quick work, but friendship is a slow ripening fruit." Even under the best circumstances, it takes time and work to develop trust with another person. How much more difficult to *rebuild* trust after it has been shattered!

Sometimes it simply isn't wise even to try. Would you ask an arsonist to housesit while you're on vacation? No thanks. Would you share your intimate secrets with someone who is a gossip? Not on your life!

As much as we may want a restored relationship, we need to use common sense to protect ourselves. The writer of Proverbs 22:3 put it plainly: "The prudent sees danger and hides himself, but the simple go on and suffer for it" (esv). Or, as *Lord of the Rings* author J.R.R. Tolkien wrote, "It does not do to leave a live dragon out of your calculations, if you live near him." [4] In other words, if you sense danger, get out of the way!

In the early years at Hope for the Heart, I encountered a situation where I needed to have firm boundaries—but didn't—in order to protect the ministry as well as myself. Our ministry was looking for someone to join our leadership team. An executive with a large well-known ministry—someone with impressive credentials—contacted me.

When "Jeff" phoned, he said he had "worked himself out of a job" by achieving his goals ahead of schedule and training several sharp people to replace him. Now he was ready for a new challenge. Besides, he said, God had told him to contact us—Hope for the Heart was the place God was sending him for his next assignment.

Smooth as polished marble, he seemed the ideal candidate and immediately joined our staff.

Jeff dived into his new responsibilities and made a strong impression with his enthusiasm and creativity. But within a couple of months, rough spots appeared on his smooth veneer.

A longtime employee asked that we speak confidentially. "Did you really tell Jeff I wasn't worth a raise?"

I was stunned. "What do you mean? I've never even had a conversation with Jeff about your salary."

"I thought so! That didn't sound like you. Jeff told me three days ago that you've been very unhappy with my work."

I affirmed this capable woman and told her not to worry.

I wondered, *Why would Jeff say something like this? Why would he want to cause this valued employee to feel so devalued?*

As time went on, more and more troublesome incidents came to my attention. The president of another organization whom I considered a friend called to say he was so sorry to hear about the "rift" between us. He hadn't known about my negative opinion of him and his ministry.

What? I had no idea what he was talking about and, indeed, felt our relationship was as strong and harmonious as ever.

He mentioned how Jeff had revealed my displeasure and my desire to sever our working relationship.

The picture became painfully clear. Jeff was manipulative, scheming, and divisive, and, over time, his shiny façade began to crack and crumble like brittle clay. He worked all the angles and pitted people against each other. Sometimes he would intentionally drive a wedge between two people, then step in to mediate, always looking like the hero. Other times he would manufacture problems so he could appear brilliant when he "fixed" them. I discovered later that he had spread insidious rumors, harming my reputation and giving the ministry a black eye. The boulders of bitterness formed by Jeff could have filled a stone quarry.

Sad to say, Jeff was a wolf in sheep's clothing. It became necessary to let him go. It was a painful parting of ways for all involved.

Not long after leaving Hope for the Heart, Jeff worked at an organization where our paths crossed occasionally at conventions. Once or twice a year for the next several years when I saw him, I prayed Psalm 141:3: "Set a guard over my mouth, O Lord; keep watch over the door of my lips." I didn't want to be guilty of doing what he had done to me. When I would pass him at meetings, I would be cordial. However, I was not eager—or even willing—to reconcile with him. I wasn't about to re-establish any kind of ongoing relationship. That decision wasn't made out of spite or bitterness, but out of common sense and an understanding of human nature.

Someone who is devious and underhanded is not whole spiritually, emotionally, or mentally. I feared that if I shared anything about myself or our ministry, he might take the information and run amok with it. To this day, when our paths cross, I choose to be respectful. But since nothing has happened to restore my trust in him, I carefully maintain a safe distance outside his stone-throwing range.

I am convinced God wants us to steer clear of stone throwers.

I don't share this story to disparage Jeff. I worked through the process of forgiveness and now hold no grudge whatsoever. I bring this up to illustrate that there are times when reconciliation *shouldn't* happen because it may cause further harm and damage.

Is There a Roadmap to Reconciliation?

We've all been wounded by others and, at some point, we've also been responsible, if only inadvertently, for causing others pain. When two people who have been at odds agree to walk the road toward reconciliation, it's helpful to know what will be required for the journey. It is also important to know what healthy, appropriate reconciliation looks like. The following map can help you prepare for every twist and turn.

The Offended: What Must You Take on the Trip?

When you've been wounded, how do you know when it's safe to seek a restored relationship? When and how should reconciliation happen? Here's a list of provisions you'll need for your trip toward reconciliation:

—*Genuine forgiveness.* Reconciliation will never succeed unless you have truly dismissed the debt against your offender—in other words, the bag of bitterness has been *thoroughly* emptied. Without your forgiveness, you and your offender are unlikely to move forward.

The Six Rays of the Star

Star sapphires have been labeled "the gem of the heavens." Ancient Persians asserted that the earth rested upon a giant sapphire, and its reflection colored the vast blue skies. The star sapphire's starlike design is known as an "asterism," a six-rayed pattern of needle-like extensions that distinguishes this gemstone from all others. Second in hardness only to diamonds, the star sapphire's strength lives up to its beauty.

Like the asterism atop a star sapphire, imagine extended across your mind the *not-so-beautiful* thoughts toward those who have hurt you. Thoughts of revenge can, in time, become engraved in your mind and darken your heart.

Your thoughts, however, must not master you. Rather, you are to master your thoughts...with the help of the Master Engraver. When you give Him your rocks of resentment, you allow Him to create a stunning new six-rayed pattern formed from *pruning* your heart of hatred, *preventing* thoughts of personal revenge, *pushing* back all thoughts of self-pity, *praying* for your offender's heart to change, *practicing* forgiving "little" wrongs, and *planting* God's Word in your mind.

This new pattern will display to all something more marvelous than the asterism atop the esteemed star sapphire—a reflection of the *mind of Christ.*

Counselor Robert Enright suggests that a halfhearted forgiveness on your part is too flimsy to support real reconciliation:

> Reconciliation without forgiveness is often no more than an armed truce in which each side patrols the demilitarized zone looking for incursions [a hostile entrance into a territory] by the other and waiting to resume hostilities. Real reconciliation might require forgiveness by both parties, because in many cases there are injuries on both sides.[5]

Reconciliation sometimes fails because you, as the injured party, have not yet done the hard work of true forgiveness. Make sure you are not still clinging to the past when you attempt to begin restoring a relationship in the present. Look for signs of rocky residue that may still be hardening your heart.

—*Humility.* Often when someone offends you, it can hurt your pride. To preserve what pride you have left, it is tempting to mentally elevate yourself above your offender, to consider yourself better than the person who harmed you. In other words, thinking of yourself as a brilliant gemstone, and your offender as a dull gray glob of cement. This may be a natural response, but it does nothing to foster the restoration of a relationship. Reconciliation will be thwarted if you hold on to your "righteous indignation."

> God forgives sin, but He doesn't pretend sin didn't happen.

Humility requires letting go of any attitude of superiority or condescension. Otherwise you draw dividing lines where none should exist. Do not forget that "all have sinned and fall short of the glory of God."[6] Even the most hurtful offenders are still just people who have, themselves, been hurt.

—*A willingness to risk.* Reconciliation is not for cowards. Two people coming together after a conflict takes hard work. To succeed, you must be willing to be vulnerable, within reason. After suffering a painful wound, many people vow never to allow themselves to be hurt again. This inner vow lets the pendulum swing too far in the opposite direction. The only way to keep such a vow is to never be in a relationship again.

There is a difference between setting boundaries and completely closing the border with an emotional iron curtain. Remain open enough to give reconciliation room to breathe and grow according to God's plan. C.S. Lewis put it this way: "To love at all is to be vulnerable.... The only place outside Heaven where you can be perfectly safe from all the dangers and perturbations of love is Hell."[7]

—*Truth and love.* Throughout the Bible, these two concepts—truth and love—run on parallel tracks. God forgives sin, but He doesn't pretend sin didn't happen. You are called by God to be "speaking the truth in love."[8]

Love, the first cousin of forgiveness, offers acceptance and mercy to the one who has wronged you. Truth does not flinch from facing reality and calling wrong *wrong*. This is a sticking point for many people who feel like forgiveness equals *enablement*. They say, "By forgiving someone who caused so much grief, aren't I just enabling him to cause more grief? Aren't I just implicitly condoning sin?"

Suppose a man borrows $500 from you and later refuses to pay back the loan. Though difficult, you can work through your feelings of betrayal and forgive him. Release him and the offense to God. A year later, should you loan this unrepentant man more money? Absolutely not. There's nothing noble or godly about giving irresponsible people another opportunity to take advantage of you. And God certainly doesn't want you to facilitate the irresponsible behavior of others. To reiterate: You can be loving (offering forgiveness) while being truthful (candidly addressing the offense) and wise (extending trust only as it is earned).

Hear me loud and clear on this point: Forgiveness is *not* enablement. Those two powerful issues need not become intertwined. You can extend grace while being completely truthful with yourself and your offender. Consider the following points:

Enablement means putting yourself in a position of being offended again and again. You can forgive the person who hurt you, but there's no reason to subject yourself to further harm. Being perpetually pelted is not part of God's plan.

Enabling never helps offenders change but further ingrains their bad habits. By overtly or silently implying it's okay when someone does wrong, you give permission for the offender to continue doing wrong. This only perpetuates a destructive pattern of pummeling.

Enablers are classic people pleasers who don't say no when they should say no. If you say yes to irresponsible people when you should say no, you are actually saying no to Christ. The apostle Paul said, "Am I now trying to win the approval of men, or of God? Or am I trying to please men? If I were still trying to please men, I would not be a servant of Christ."[9]

By being an enabler, you may be subverting God's will for your life as well as for your offender's life. Many times we must say no to people so we can say yes to God.

The Offender: What Must You Take on the Trip?

You'll need a very different set of provisions for the trip toward reconciliation when you have been the person responsible—inadvertently or not—for wounding another. These include:

—*Demonstrate genuine repentance.* Everyone has received a half-hearted apology at some point. Nothing is as unsatisfying as a begrudging, "All right, *if* I did anything wrong, I'm sorry," which is only meant to pacify the accuser and get the guilty person off the hook. Sure, it's tough to come clean about a failure or blatant offense, and many people are reluctant to admit guilt. They say, "Maybe I did kind of flub up." Maybe? Kind of? Flub up? How about this instead: "I admit I made a terrible mistake by lying to you. I behaved deceitfully and immaturely, and I did not show you the respect you deserve. I was wrong. Would you forgive me for my actions?"[10]

False repentance and hollow apologies do nothing to rebuild trust. This insightful scripture contrasts the false with the true:

"Godly sorrow brings repentance that leads to salvation and leaves no regret, but worldly sorrow brings death."[11]

As the offending party, you have *no right to expect reconciliation* until repentance has been verified by observable consistent behavior over a substantial period of time. Anything less makes trust impossible.

—*Acknowledge causing pain.* Unlike forgiveness, which requires no response from the offender, reconciliation calls for the recognition and admission of painful offenses. What a huge step you will take toward healing when you say, "I know what I did hurt you. Although I can't possibly understand the extent of pain I've caused, I do realize that I've wounded you. I now see the damage caused by my actions."

Failing to acknowledge the hurt you've caused may mean you are in denial—that you are unwilling to face the full consequences and ramifications of your offenses. Refusal to accept responsibility for inflicting pain blocks reconciliation, whereas owning up to the hardship caused helps facilitate it.

—*Make full restitution.* To restore a relationship, you must be willing to repair the damage your actions caused and provide tangible repayment, if at all possible. Think about the story of Zacchaeus. As Jesus was passing through Jericho one day, the rich tax collector wanted to get a glimpse of Him. But he was too short, so he climbed a tree to see over the crowd. When Jesus reached the tree, He looked up and said, "Zacchaeus, hurry and come down, for I must stay at your house today." That surprised everyone—including Zacchaeus. Tax collectors were despised because they grew rich by cheating people. But Zacchaeus was so moved by Jesus' message of mercy and forgiveness that he declared, "Behold, Lord, the half of my goods I give to the poor. And if I have defrauded anyone of anything, I restore it fourfold." Jesus offered him forgiveness. Zacchaeus responded with *restitution* for what he had stolen.[12]

If trust is to be rebuilt, you must "put your money where your mouth is." In extreme offenses, this may be impossible (such as a death caused by a drunk driver), which makes reconciliation exceedingly difficult. But where possible, you must return what's taken—repay stolen money, repair damaged property, correct hurtful gossip. Any tangible act of restitution is a "good faith" sign of contrition.

—*Establish personal accountability.* For reconciliation to work, you must not only accept responsibility for past actions, but also accept accountability for future ones. Depending upon the seriousness of the offense, the person you've hurt may need to set a boundary by insisting that you be answerable to a third party.

Christian psychiatrist and author Dr. Paul Meier says,

> Every human alive should be accountable to at least one other human. Whoever thinks he doesn't need accountability needs it the most. The apostle Paul was an outstanding believer, but he was always accountable and never traveled alone. He usually took Dr. Luke along with him, and often Silas, Barnabas or others as well. Paul said that we should really worry when we think we *can't fail* because that's exactly when we *will fail*. It was also Paul who said he sometimes did what he didn't want to do and didn't do some things he wished he would have done.[13]

In other words, even an exceptional Christian like the apostle Paul needed accountability.

Suppose a husband confesses to his wife that he's had an extramarital affair. He seems genuinely contrite and ashamed. Through a long process—saturated with disbelief, anger, and sadness—the wife comes to a point of forgiveness. She insists, however, that they see a marriage counselor for a minimum of six months. The husband insists, on the other hand, that counseling is unnecessary. In fact, he refuses to go.

"I've apologized dozens of times, and I've fully admitted how stupid I was. We don't need some counselor poking around in our business! We can handle this on our own."

What should his wife do? She should be wary and watchful. If her husband is unwilling to accept accountability, in all probability, the same issues that led him into a first affair will lead him into a second.[14]

If you're asked to be held accountable, it shouldn't be done punitively. The message shouldn't be, "Because I suffered, you're going to suffer too by attending weekly meetings with your accountability group, or having a counselor ask pointed questions that make you squirm."

The intent of accountability is to help you change, grow, and improve. This is why you should willingly submit to being held accountable—the person you hurt needs to better understand the motivation behind your hurtful behavior in order to avoid repeating it.

If you're evaluating whether or not you need accountability, keep in mind Dr. Meier's observation: "Whoever thinks he doesn't need accountability needs it the most."

≈

Two months after my phone conversation with Clint—the rejected husband who was confused regarding reconciliation—he sent me a follow-up e-mail. I was happy to hear from him, because I had been wondering whether or not he decided to reconcile with Vicky.

"I've been meeting with my pastor and continuing with my church support group. They all told me the same thing you told me: Reconciliation would be possible and even honorable, but it can only work under certain conditions. After much prayer and soul-searching, I've decided not to get back together with Vicky.

> God never expects us to put ourselves in harm's way when someone who hurt us shows no remorse.

Why? The deciding factor was that she resisted—and then outright refused—to get help for addiction. She said she had beat it once on her own, years ago, and she could do it again. Hello! She never beat her addiction to begin with. Clearly, she is blinded to the truth about herself and unwilling to look honestly at her problems."

Clint went on to emphasize that he has forgiven Vicky and is trying to maintain a friendly, supportive relationship with her. But for his sake and his children's—and even Vicky's—there is no way he would go back to the way things were. Too much had happened and, most importantly, too many problems had resurfaced in Vicky's life that she wasn't willing to address.

Although I much prefer a happily-ever-after ending, I admire Clint for standing his ground and holding appropriate boundaries. After all, forgiveness is free of charge, but reconciliation requires a hefty investment from those involved. God never expects us to put ourselves in harm's way when someone who hurt us shows no sign of remorse, repentance, or change.

Emptying your bag of emotional boulders may or may not involve reconciliation. In fact, establishing ground rules for your relationships may actually enhance your odds of having healthy reconciliation and keep you from enabling an offender to hurt you over and over. It forces violators to earn your trust with tangible action, not just words.

God is pleased when reconciliation occurs between two people—when both empty their bags of their boulders. But if your offender is unwilling to forgive, your bag can still be boulder-free.

10

Breaking the Power of Your Pelter

Praying for Those Who Pelt You

No one likes being duped, and we certainly don't like admitting it when it happens to us. I, of course, am no exception. But to be candid, I have not only been duped, but big-time duped! At least I learned valuable lessons through that difficult and humbling experience.

Well over 20 years ago I was contacted by an evangelist who had moved to my hometown and my home church. Over the phone, he shared that he had just preached a series of church meetings at which God had deeply moved in the hearts of the people. I thought that was wonderful. Then "Dan" described his ministry plans and all his upcoming opportunities to preach. Then he asked if we could meet in person—as soon as possible. I responded yes, and he came to my home immediately.

"I'm excited about these ministry opportunities, but I have a problem. I hate to admit it, but money is tight right now...and I need to buy food for my family!" Dan handed me a photograph of his beautiful wife and two young children. "It's been a tough time for us, but we know the hand of the Lord is on our ministry. Clearly, we are in God's will. If you would loan me $300, I should receive a check in three or four days to cover it. I'll pay you back as soon as the check arrives."

Call me a sucker for cute kids and a longsuffering wife. To say nothing of my desire not to thwart God's will.

I wrote out a check for $300, and Dan assured me again that it was a loan he would pay back. He left, promising he'd be in touch soon with a progress report.

Dan returned to my office a month later asking for additional funds. Things were going well, he said, and exciting plans were in motion. The Lord was at work!

I wrote another check.

This went on for a few more months, and each time Dan told me he'd keep me up to date with regular progress reports. I never calculated how much money I "loaned" him, and I really don't want to know.

Then several months passed without contact from Dan and, frankly, not much thought about him on my part. Finally, I received a wholly unexpected progress report: Dan was in prison. To this day, I'm unclear about the reasons for his incarceration.

In the meantime, I was able to meet Dan's wife and children, and they were as delightful as advertised. His wife was angelic, and his children as sweet as they could be. I helped them get into an apartment and took food to them on numerous occasions. They were genuinely grateful and kindhearted, and I came to like them very much.

In fact, this woman turned out to be conscientious and responsible. When I called her at one point to see if they needed financial help, she declined my offer, explaining that she had found a job and was managing to make ends meet.

Two years passed and Dan was released from prison. Not surprisingly, I received a call and we scheduled a meeting.

He said he hadn't been able to find a job yet. A bit wiser this time around, I suggested that maybe he should take a temporary job bagging groceries or hauling furniture—anything to provide some money to pay bills and stay afloat.

He was indignant. "Why, I could never do anything of the sort! I have a certain image to maintain, after all."

I told Dan gently that I would be unable to provide any more money.

He persisted, saying that his kids needed clothes and his wife could barely put food on the table. That definitely hit my soft spot, but again, I said no.

As he stormed out of my office, he hissed over his shoulder, "And you call yourself a Christian!"

That was the last I heard from Dan.

As you can imagine, I had a barrage of *bad* feelings and several sizeable stones of indignation dropped into my bag. I had been the victim of a scam, and I felt deceived and duped. I felt sorry for Dan's wife and kids. I felt naïve for having enabled his irresponsible behavior. I felt mad at Dan for using me—and others, as it turned out—to get money on false pretenses.

Still stewing the following week, a certain Bible passage reverberated in my head as if someone were leaning on the doorbell of my house: "Love your enemies, bless those who curse you, do good to those who hate you, and pray for those who spitefully use you and persecute you."[1] No doubt about it—I felt spitefully used. In truth, I wanted a thunderbolt from heaven to zap him!

Apparently God was giving me a refresher course in a lesson I thought I'd learned a year before. At that time, I'd been deeply hurt by a family member who had said many cruel things about my mother and me. One day, during my devotional time, I prayed, "God, I don't know what to do. I can't change this situation. Show me how to respond." A short time later, I saw a scripture I had never seen before: "As for me, far be it from me that I should sin against the LORD by failing to pray for you."[2]

The truth is, I had not been praying for this person—nor had the thought even crossed my mind. But by faith, I began praying, and healing started to happen—in our relationship and in my heart. Consistent prayer sanded my jagged rocks of resentment into smooth stones, and before long they disintegrated and my bag was emptied.

Now, a year later, God gave me the same instructions: Forgive Dan *and* pray for him.

This is where the difficulty with forgiveness gets ratcheted up considerably. It's no wonder many people become resistant when presented with Christ's command to pray for their enemies, "You want me to do *what?* Pray for the person who harmed me? That's asking too much."

I understand that rationale. I used to chafe against the very notion. It runs counter to our nature and will. From a human standpoint, praying for enemies seems impossible. But the Bible says, "With God nothing will be impossible."[3] God often asks us to do things that go against our natural way of thinking and feeling.

The command to pray for those who hurt us can be confusing and a real roadblock on the journey of forgiveness. Jesus gave us the command, but what did He mean? And why would He tell us to do that?

How Do We Pray for Our Enemies?

Someone said that forgiving an offender is letting go of the wish for bad things to happen to him, while prayer is the desire for good things to happen to him. That's *partially* true, and the difficulty in praying for someone often stems from a misunderstanding about this point.

The Greek word *agape*, translated "love" in the Matthew 5 passage about praying for your enemies, intrinsically means "a commitment to seek the highest good of another person." The "highest good" for those who are genuinely wrong is that their hearts become genuinely right. So the intent is not for us to pray that our offender would receive blessings from God, such as more money, more power, more prestige, and all the rest. No, we are to pray for that person's "highest good," which first of all means salvation in Christ and, if that person is already a believer, to be transformed into the character of Christ. We pray not that the Lord will *prosper* that person, but that He will cause growth and maturity. We pray that whatever prompted our enemy to harm us—pride, arrogance, selfishness, deceit—will be addressed by God in His way and in His time.

With all this in mind, I began praying:

> *Heavenly Father, you know that Dan needs a changed life. He needs a changed heart. I pray that You will bring to him the circumstances or people or whatever it takes to soften his heart. I pray that You would mold him into a man of integrity—a man his wife can respect and his children can admire. May he see his need for You and turn to You to change his life. In Jesus' name I pray. Amen.*

I found in this situation—and others similar to it—that prayer totally redirected my heart. I looked at Dan's *need* instead of his *fault*, as my mother had so beautifully modeled for me with my dad. I saw him as a flawed man whose heart could be changed by God. His spiritual life was missing what only the Lord could give.

> Prayer redirects our hearts—we focus on the *need* instead of the *fault*.

If Dan was willing, God would make him whole. My prayer helped grind away the stones of indignation weighing heavy on my heart.

Every time I thought of Dan, every time I saw him, every time I was reminded of him, I went to God in prayer. As a result, those prayers—looking beyond his fault and seeing his need—helped change my heart.

What Are the Benefits of Praying for Our Enemies?

Notice praying for your enemy is commanded by Christ—it's not optional. God wants us to pray for our enemies so that His highest good may be achieved in their lives.

Our enemies are like geodes, rough and rugged on the outside with no apparent beauty—a type of rock we'd leave behind if we found one. But God knows the potential that lies within, and over time, something extraordinary can be created. Split open a craggy geode and what do you find inside? Crystals.

There are other reasons Jesus gave us this command as well.

Prayer Insulates Us from Bitterness

When we pray for the spiritual growth of our enemy, a change occurs within our hearts. Firsthand I have experienced that, when I pray, even if my enemy doesn't change, *I change.* Through prayer, our hearts and minds are aligned with God's heart and mind (see Appendix G on page 211).

You can't pray for someone consistently—and the key word is *consistently*—without developing compassion for that person. Through prayer, the Holy Spirit softens the hardened pieces of our hearts, hatred is turned to love, the bitter is turned to sweet. We begin to see even our enemies through God's eyes.

Prayer stirs all those seemingly immovable rocks and boulders in our burlap bag.

The apostle Peter wrote, "Do not repay evil with evil or insult with insult, but with blessing, because to this you were called so that you may inherit a blessing." He went on to quote from Psalm 34: "For, whoever would love life and see good days must keep his tongue from evil and his lips from deceitful speech. He must turn from evil and do good; he must seek peace and pursue it."[4] Part of the blessing we inherit is peace of heart and mind. When we bless others with our prayers, we are blessed in return. The Holy Spirit removes our bitterness so we can experience the blessing of God.

Prayer Allows Us to Be Controlled by the Spirit, Not the Offender

When Janine pulled me aside after I'd spoken on forgiveness, she said, "I've really tried to forgive my ex-husband for betraying me and our kids. He ran out on us two years ago without warning. Turns out he'd been having an affair with a co-worker who is ten years younger than he is. Now they're living together—at least, that's the last I heard."

Janine struggled to hold back tears as she spoke, still sore and aching from boulders of bitterness that pummeled her two years ago.

"I've come a long way in letting go of my hatred toward him. And that was tough because he's such a domineering and overbearing person. He ruled our house with an iron fist. He was totally controlling."

Then she got to the crux of the matter: "June, I've forgiven him, but I can't bring myself to pray for him. Every time his face shows up in my mind, when I sit down to pray, I totally shut down. I can't go on."

We talked for a while, and I tried to comfort Janine, who was obviously having difficulty getting her boulders to budge. Then I mentioned something she hadn't considered.

"Janine, you said your husband was controlling and how hard that was for you."

She nodded.

"Well, it might be that he's *still* controlling you."

A scowl formed on her face. She didn't like the sound of that.

"When we hold on to bitterness toward someone who hurt us, we give power to that person. Negative emotions are natural. Pain is a human response when we are wronged. But that pain can cause us to act in a way that we would not choose. As a result, we allow our actions to be dictated by the other person's offense."

I told her that I've heard of many cases in which an abandoned wife moved to a different town—leaving behind friends, job, church—just to get away from the man who betrayed her. He stays put while her whole life is disrupted. Or consider the person who is the target of nasty gossip. The victim chooses to leave and go somewhere else to avoid whispers and pointing fingers. Meanwhile, the gossipmonger stays there, probably glad to have the other person out of the way.

> What freedom when Christ—rather than a person—controls our thoughts and actions.

It's understandable why those wounded individuals would choose to leave—but still, they are being controlled by the wrongdoer. They are allowing their actions to be shaped by the person who caused them harm.

The same principle applies to prayer. When we refuse to pray for our enemy, we give power to that person. The offender is still controlling what we do. Every time Janine tried to pray for her husband, toxic feelings bubbled up within her, keeping her from doing what she wanted to do.

I say all this not to heap guilt on you if you're struggling to pray for your enemy. None of us want to hear that our offender is controlling us. Forgiveness is a process, and it can take a long time to be able to pray for someone who has deeply wounded you. But understand that we *can* turn control of our lives over to God and do His will. We *can* learn to pray, then forgive, even when we don't feel like it.

There is tremendous freedom when Christ—rather than a person—controls our thoughts and actions.

Supernatural Prayer: Chris's Story

It was five days before Christmas when a stranger approached ten-year-old Christopher Carrier, claiming to be a friend of his father.

"I want to buy him a gift, and I need your help."

Eager to do something nice for his dad's friend, Chris climbed into a motor home parked up the street.

The driver took Chris to a remote field, claiming to be lost, and asked Chris to look at a map. Suddenly, Chris felt a sharp pain in his back. The stranger had stabbed him with an ice pick. The man drove the wounded boy down a dirt road, shot him in the left temple, and left him for dead in the alligator-infested Florida Everglades.

Chris lay lifeless for six days until someone driving by spotted him. Chris miraculously survived his injuries, though he was left blind in one eye. Because he was unable to identify his attacker, police could not make an arrest. For a long time, young Chris remained terrified, despite police protection.

Some time later, his life took another dramatic turn—this time a positive one. Friends took him to a church youth group and there, Chris trusted Jesus as his Savior.

"I was overwhelmed with emotion because I knew I had never personally accepted the Savior."

This turning point in Chris's life came three years after the attack. Later, at age 15, Chris shared his story for the first time. He eventually decided to pursue full-time ministry and help others find the peace he had discovered in Christ.

More than a decade later, a detective phoned Chris to tell him that a man had confessed to the crime that had cost him sight in his left eye—and nearly his life. The man's name was David McAllister. Chris made plans to visit the frail and now blind man, who was living in a nursing home. The strong man Chris remembered abducting him was now a broken and weak 77-year-old.

Chris learned from the detective some of the details behind what had happened years earlier. McAllister had been hired by Chris's father to work as a nurse for an ailing uncle. Chris's dad had caught McAllister drinking on the job and had fired him. The senseless attack on Chris had been motivated by revenge.

As Chris now talked to the old man, McAllister denied knowing anything about the kidnapping. Then as Chris revealed more about himself, the old man softened and eventually apologized.

"What you meant for evil, God has turned into a wonderful blessing." Chris told his attacker how God had allowed his wounds to become open doors to share the good news of Christ.

Chris went home and told his wife and kids about meeting the man who had tried to kill him. The entire family began praying for McAllister and making almost daily visits to his nursing home. During one Sunday afternoon visit, Chris posed the most important question he had yet asked McAllister: "Do you want to know the Lord?" McAllister said yes, and Chris led him in a prayer of salvation.

A few days later, McAllister died in his sleep.

Chris says it is not a story of regret, but of redemption. His story illustrates the life-changing power of an empty bag.

"I saw the Lord give that man back his life, and so much more. I can't wait to see him again someday—in heaven."

≈

If you're like me, you hear stories such as this and think, *How in the world could someone forgive and pray for a man who tried to murder him in a vicious, coldhearted manner? How is that possible?*

You might be asking these questions in regard to your own life.

Jesus provides the only answer we can rely on: "With man this is impossible, but with God all things are possible."[5]

Going the extra mile in the area of forgiveness may seem a tall order. And it is. But God never asks us to do anything without supplying us the strength to accomplish it. If praying for those who persecute you seems too hard, just remember: "Everything is possible for him who believes."[6]

11

Blindsided by a God-sized Boulder

"Oh God, How Could You Allow This?"

EVERY DAY, CHARLES PARKED his milk truck at the only place in the neighborhood where there was room for it: in the gravel lot across from the one-room West Nickel Mines Amish school. The students knew him, and he knew their families.

An average guy, Charles lived in an ordinary house with his wife, Marie, and their three young children. He worked the night shift as a milk truck driver in an Amish community in Pennsylvania, collecting milk from local dairy farms. Neighbors described him as a devoted father. He found time to jump on the trampoline with his kids and to drive them faithfully to sports practices.

He walked them to the school bus every weekday morning. Marie attended a mothers' prayer circle that gathered regularly to ask God to protect the children of the community. No one knew the pain Charles felt. No one realized that unresolved bitterness was slowly leading him to commit unspeakable violence.

Charles Roberts was angry at God—*very* angry. His emotional bag was stretched beyond capacity.

On Monday, October 2, 2006, he left the truck as usual at 3:00 a.m. and went home. Later that day, he was supposed to go to the office for a drug screening, a routine occurrence for drivers of big rigs in Pennsylvania. But Charles never intended to keep his appointment. By the time he put his kids on the school bus that morning, he had already written four suicide notes—one for each member of his family.

From the bus stop, he drove to the hardware store to purchase a few supplies he still lacked. He already had the guns. He needed more nylon ties for binding hostages.

Shortly after 10:30 a.m., Charles entered the Amish school building, his emotional bag bulging with pent-up pressure. He was armed with a 9mm handgun, a shotgun, a stun gun, and 600 rounds of ammunition. He immediately ordered all 15 boys to leave the school, along with the 20-year-old teacher and several other adult women visiting the class. That left him alone with ten young girls, ages 6-13. He forced them to stand facing the blackboard while he tied their ankles together. The teacher, Emma Mae Zook, ran to a nearby farmhouse to call the police.

Officers arrived at the school within minutes. Seeing them outside, Charles called Marie on a cell phone. He told her about the suicide notes. He told her he would not be coming home.

He then called 911 and threatened to kill the girls if the police didn't leave within "two seconds." *Stretched and timeworn, his bag began ripping apart...*

The dispatcher tried to keep Charles on the phone long enough to transfer the call to officers on the scene, but Charles hung up and quickly carried out his threat. The bag burst apart and Charles shot all ten girls, killing five of them. When the gunfire erupted, police stormed the building. Charles fatally shot himself as they entered the room.

For 20 years, Charles carried secret, submerged guilt that tormented and angered him. When he was 12, he molested two young girls—members of his family. Years later, he began to have nightmares about "doing it again."

On top of that anguish, in 1997, Charles and Marie lost their first child at birth. The tiny girl was premature and lived only 20 minutes. Her death crushed his spirit, and he never recovered. He blamed God for cutting the baby's life short.

Nine years after that excruciating loss, Charles's buried anger finally took its toll. The rage inside his emotional bag exploded, propelling sharp, jagged rock fragments throughout an entire community—shattering lives. He made a fateful decision that dramatically altered the lives of hundreds of people forever. His suicide note stated:

> [The baby's death] changed my life forever, I haven't been the same since. It affected me in a way I never felt possible. I am filled with so much hate, hate towards myself, hate towards God and unimaginable emptiness. It seems like every time we do something fun, I think about how Elise wasn't here to share it with us and I got right back to anger.[1]

Where Was God?

Events that morning left the entire nation in a state of shock. It was the third deadly school shooting in the span of a week. Yet this time was different. It is hard to imagine a more peaceful, sheltered environment than an Amish schoolhouse. Deeply religious people, the Amish shun modern technology, including televisions, cars, and electricity. They purposefully live a simple, agrarian existence that insulates them from the frantic pace of modern American life along with its chaos and violence.

The thought of mass murder intruding on such unspoiled innocence was too much, even for Americans desensitized to violence by a steady diet of gruesome news and "entertainment." All over the country, people immediately started asking the age-old questions: "Why? Where was God? How could He allow such a horrible thing to happen?"

Why didn't God stop the rage in Charles's bag from exploding so violently?

Everyone—Christians included—wanted to know how the senseless murder of young school girls fits the vision of God as a loving and protective Father.

Ironically, the contents of Charles's suicide note suggests he was plagued by the very same questions. He wondered why God took his innocent baby girl from him years ago. He blamed God for his guilt and pain. Anger mangled his mind and massive boulders of bitterness triggered a landslide of heartbreaking atrocities.

Evil and Suffering: Why?

I can't begin to count the number of times people have said to me, "How could God allow this to happen? Where was He? Why didn't He intervene?" Thankfully, the vast majority of hurting, wounded people do not allow their bitterness to consume them in the same way that Charles's anger consumed him. But still, many people are deeply embittered and harbor sustained, seething anger toward God, believing that He *could* have and *should* have shielded them or someone they love from harm.

> Holding God responsible for our pain is as unproductive as it is unwise.

While they won't go so far as to say that God "sinned" by not averting tragedy, they still blame God, leaving boulders of bitterness lodged for a lifetime. Subtly or overtly they hold God responsible, continually thinking, *You may not have caused this terrible thing to happen, but You allowed it—and that's just as bad.* There was a time when I had similar thoughts, and you may have had such thoughts, too.

For true healing to occur, we need to rethink what we believe about the nature and purpose of suffering and about the sovereignty of God in our lives. Our misconceptions rob us of the opportunity to grow through difficult and painful times. Holding God responsible for our pain is as misguided as it is unproductive. It is just as harmful as refusing to forgive another person—perhaps even more so. To see our neighbors as cruel and unjust is one matter, but to see God that way drains our lives of hope and leads to deep despair.

Why Did God Create Free Will?

God could have created a world without suffering. He could have populated it with exact copies of Himself, "clones" who would never do any harm or cause any trouble. No greed, no malice, no addiction, no jealousy, no hatred. Then no one would ever ask, "How could a loving God have allowed such a horrible thing?"

But God didn't do that because, in such a world, not much of anything *could* happen. We would be like God's marionettes, with Him standing over us pulling our strings. We would do everything He wants only because we could do nothing else. Or God would be nothing more than an inventor of robots that had computer chips within that predetermined our every response. That would surely be safe and secure…but also predictable and programmed.

That is not the world God created. When He made people, He wanted more than clones, puppets, or robots. He chose to create people with whom He could have a personal relationship. He created thinking, creative people with whom He could interact throughout eternity. To accomplish this, He decided to add the most dangerous ingredient of all to our person: *free will*. For better or worse, we get to choose how we live.

We are made in God's image and have the capability and potential to be like Him, but there is no guarantee we will. Sometimes people choose right; sometimes they choose wrong. Every time someone chooses love over hate, or mercy over vengeance, good multiplies, and the world is a better place. But free will means people are just as free to make bad choices. It permits sin and rebellion to multiply, which will always result in pain and suffering. Sometimes we are victims of the bad choices of others. We are often surprised by this, but we shouldn't be. God never promised us a pain-free life. The Bible says, "Do not think it strange concerning the fiery trial which is to try you, as though some strange thing happened to you."[2] When it comes to spiritual growth, "painful trials" are where the real work gets done.

Sandblasting is a process whereby rocks are cleaned by a powerful stream of sand blown by compressed air. What looks damaging or detrimental to the rocks actually works toward refining and polishing them. God uses "big" trials—large, abrasive particles of sand, and "little" trials—softer, smoother grains, to refine and polish our character.

Consider the hardship endured by Tom, who called *Hope in the Night* not long after he brought his 17-year-old daughter, Sophie, home from the hospital. She had barely survived an overdose of the latest "recreational" drug. Tom and his wife were devastated and deeply shaken.

"I've been a Christian for twenty years, but right now I don't understand God at all! I've prayed for Him to protect Sophie every day since she was born. Where was His protection in all this? I've been faithful, but it seems to me like He wasn't."

I assured Tom that his feelings were normal—and a natural response to a heartbreaking situation. Then I added, "God *is* faithful, even though we don't always see it. And just because we ask for God's protection doesn't mean bad things won't happen to us."

Tom was quiet on the other end of the line, and I knew he was mulling this over.

"People are free to make bad choices at any time. God grieves for us when we make mistakes that hurt ourselves, or when other people make mistakes that hurt us. He doesn't always protect us *physically*—after all, He chose not to intervene when His own Son was crucified. But He does protect us *emotionally* and *spiritually*. He protects our hearts and always holds out hope for complete emotional and spiritual healing."

I told Tom that we can either have free will as humans or we can have programmed, foolproof protection as robots, but not both. We cannot have it both ways. By allowing free will along with our poor choices—or the poor choices of others—God gives us a priceless gift: the opportunity to grow, to mature, to gain wisdom, to recognize our total dependence on Him.

Many months later Tom told me the next chapter in his family's story. Before her experience with drugs, Sophie had defiantly told her parents she was sick of their "stone age" beliefs and values. She had a right, she insisted, to her own opinions about drugs, alcohol, sex, and everything else.

But after her overdose and brush with death, she decided her parents weren't so old-fashioned and uptight as she'd thought. In fact, she even joined a campus group that warns kids about the danger of drugs, and she reconnected with her church youth group. One night of pain and fear taught Sophie what a thousand parental lectures never could, and the rough edges were being smoothed.

"She is so much stronger emotionally and spiritually than she was before that awful incident. God was protecting her heart after all. I wouldn't want to go through that mess again, but now that we're on this side of it, I'm actually glad it happened."

Could Pain Have a Higher Purpose?

The main reason we see suffering as unfair—and blame God for it—is that we misunderstand the *purpose* of life. We live in a culture of comfort. We believe it is our birthright to live happy, healthy, prosperous, cushy lives. Pain of any kind is our sworn enemy. Pharmaceutical profits alone reveal the premium we place on a pain-free existence, not to mention alcohol sales and a host of illegal substances used to numb our pain. We fill our homes with comforts and conveniences. The world we've built is antiseptic, air-conditioned, and automated.

There is nothing intrinsically wrong with that way of living. The problem arises when we make comfort the aim and ambition of our existence. Comfort was never meant to be our purpose. C.S. Lewis said, "If you look for truth, you may find comfort in the end; if you look for comfort you will not get either comfort or truth— only soft soap and wishful thinking to begin with and, in the end, despair."[3]

It is clear that God's agenda is quite different from ours. He is in the business of "soul shaping," teaching us to be like Him and at times stepping into the role of Master Sandblaster. God gave us the freedom to choose how we live, and ever since Adam and Eve chose the way of rebellion, we've had the same propensity. God has forgiven us, but also desires reconciliation with us. For that to happen, we must learn to make a different choice. We must see for ourselves that something is not right with the world. It doesn't function the way God intended.

To reverse the course requires radical transformation. Like any powerful chemical reaction, this takes heat, pressure, and a catalyst to start the chain reaction. Pain can provide these things. Philip Yancey wrote:

> C.S. Lewis introduced the phrase "pain, the megaphone of God." "God whispers to us in our pleasures, speaks in our conscience, but shouts in our pains," he said; "it is His megaphone to rouse a deaf world." The word *megaphone* is apropos, because by its nature pain shouts. When I stub my toe or twist an ankle, pain loudly announces to my brain that something is wrong. Similarly, the existence of suffering on this earth is, I believe, a scream to all of us that something is wrong. It halts us in our tracks and forces us to consider other values.[4]

But why does pain have to *hurt* so much? Couldn't God halt us in our tracks some easier way? Probably not, because if He could, He would. Researchers have discovered that pain is, as Yancey says, "the gift that no one wants." We hate pain, but without it we would likely do far more harm to ourselves.

This was confirmed in a study about leprosy. For centuries we have known lepers suffer from hideous deformities that grow worse as the disease progresses. This largely accounts for how feared they have been through history. But what people didn't know for a long time is that the misshapen parts of a leper's body are not the work of the disease itself. Rather, they result from wounds the sufferers inadvertently inflict on themselves.

Why? Because leprosy destroys a person's ability to feel pain. Lepers often put their hands in scalding water without giving the heat a second thought. Not feeling any pain, they experience severe burns and blisters. When left untreated, severe infection occurs, which then results in the loss of limbs—fingers, toes, hands, feet.

> Pain is part of a vital warning system that helps us recover from our wounds—and avoid worse ones.

Dr. Paul Brand, a physician who spent his life working with lepers and saw the debilitating effects of painlessness, enthusiastically declared, "Thank God for inventing pain!"[5]

In other words, pain is not an evil to be avoided at all costs. It is part of a vital warning system that helps us recover from our wounds—and avoid worse ones. Furthermore, it is necessary for pain to *really* hurt, or we would just ignore its message and miss its refining effect.

Job, known for his forbearance in suffering, became well familiar with divine purpose in pain. "He knows the way that I take; when he has tested me, I will come forth as gold."[6]

In the case of physical pain, the point is obvious. If I break my arm and fail to get it set by a skilled physician, it won't heal properly, and I will have worse problems later on. The principle is just as true when we experience pain from emotional or psychological brokenness. The pain is a messenger warning something needs to be "set right." We need the Great Physician to mend our broken hearts and, at times, perform surgery on our damaged emotions so we might experience full healing.

Hurt as the Impetus for Healing: Dolores's Story

Dolores, now in her fifties, called *Hope in the Night* one evening because she was tired of tiptoeing around an emotional wound that wouldn't heal. When she was young, her parents were dirt-poor and had no hope of sending all four of their children to college. Dolores desperately wanted to study veterinary medicine. As the oldest child, she felt entitled to receive the education. She always earned top marks in school and proved herself to be a bright and diligent student.

Dolores's parents were immigrants with Old World ideas about the role of women in society. Her younger brother was chosen to go to college instead, while she stayed home. Dolores, deeply disappointed and disheartened, deposited into her emotional bag a rock of resentment against her brother. She never let go of that injustice and held it against him for years, even though she knew it wasn't his fault.

"I eventually put myself through school, which was very empowering. But to this day I can't be near my brother without feeling the same horrible hurt I experienced the day he left home. I know it's irrational, but that's how I feel."

This persistent pain served as God's call for Dolores to forgive. Upon realizing this, she took steps to make peace with her past and with her brother. It required several conversations, but the two were able to move past the hostility that had divided them for so long.

As a result, Dolores's bag felt "light as a feather."

Because ours is a culture of comfort, few of us would go as far as Dr. Brand to declare, "Thank God for inventing pain!" But the apostle Paul went even further. He considers the knowledge we gain by suffering to be so valuable that he tells us to be *happy* about it:

> We also rejoice in our sufferings, because we know that suffering produces perseverance; perseverance, character; and character, hope. And hope does not disappoint us, because God has poured out his love into our hearts by the Holy Spirit, whom he has given us.[7]

In other words, our suffering is never in vain. Its purpose is to produce endurance, character, hope, and love. It gives us the chance to learn, mature, and improve. So suffering is worthwhile. Instead of asking, "How could God let this happen?" consider asking, "How can I harness this pain and use it to make me more Christlike? What do I need to do to heal these wounds?" In other words, what is the *point* of this pain?

Turning blame and bitterness into healing and hope can take a long time. Some of us have suffered unrelenting offenses, years of horrific abuse. If so, we may have to measure progress one millimeter at a time. Thankfully, we have permission to take our time. God knows even the smallest step away from resentment is a step toward freedom. Chiseling away at the rocks of rancor is indeed progress.

What Is the Faith Factor?

Whether we succeed depends on our willingness to exercise our faith in God, to *trust* Him, even when we must draw upon every ounce of energy and hold on to the thinnest of threads. The fact is, we may never understand the higher purpose God has in mind for our suffering, or get to see our pain bear fruit. But again, stuffing our bags with rocks, stones, and boulders is never part of God's plan—for any of us.

Sometimes Paul's comforting words must simply be taken by faith: "We know that all things work together for good to those who love God, to those who are the called according to His purpose."[8]

That's easy enough to say at a safe distance. Sometimes it's easier recited than applied. Let's turn again to Job, who is a model for trusting God even through the most intense suffering. This unsuspecting man was hit with every tragedy imaginable. He lost his family, his fortune, and his health. The situation was so bad that his wife snarled, "Curse God and die." His friends sat on the ground with him for seven days and seven nights without saying a word, so great was his suffering. When they did speak, they blamed him: *Your calamity is because of your sin.*

In the end, after pouring out his bitter complaints to God, Job had only one hope left to stand on: his faith in the character and goodness

Blaming God for our suffering looks back and focuses on our pain. Trusting God looks forward and focuses on His plan.

of God. He said, "I know that you can do all things; no plan of yours can be thwarted.... My ears had heard of you but now my eyes have seen you. Therefore I despise myself and repent in dust and ashes."[9]

Through all his suffering, Job moved from *hearing* about God to *seeing* God, and ultimately to *experiencing* God in deepened fellowship.

Blaming God for our suffering looks backward and focuses on our pain. *Trusting God* looks forward and focuses on His plan. By trusting, we assume God really does have a purpose—one that is always for our good—whether we can see it at the time or not.

An old Chinese story reminds us that we are not wise enough to know how God's plan for our lives will unfold. Once there was a man who lived in the countryside with his only son. They were simple peasants, eking out a living on a small farm. One day, their only horse broke free and ran away. Now, without a horse, they would have to do all the farm work by hand.

All the neighbors gathered around. "That's terrible," they said.

But the old man had been around a long time and had learned a thing or two about God's ways.

"How do you know?" he asked.

The next day, a miracle happened. The lost horse returned and brought ten wild horses with it. The man and his son were suddenly rich by peasant standards.

"That's wonderful!" said the neighbors at the celebration party.

The old man just pulled at his beard and said, "How do you know?"

The next day, the son tried to ride one of the wild horses. He fell to the ground and broke his leg. The father was too old to tame the animals himself, so their good fortune seemed to fade as quickly as it had arrived.

The neighbors visited with flowers and food. "That's horrible!" they said.

They didn't understand the old man at all when he said again, "How do you know?"

The following day, the whole country went to war. All the able-bodied men were sent into battle, and only one in ten came home again. Because of his broken leg, the son was spared.

The old cliché "God works in mysterious ways" is never more true than when we try to understand our suffering. But just because God's purpose is sometimes a mystery doesn't mean He doesn't have a purpose. Nothing escapes His attention or happens outside His control.

Faith in Action: The Nickel Mines Story

In October 2006, the eyes of the world were riveted on a remote one-room schoolhouse in Pennsylvania. In typical fashion, the news media told and retold the story of Charles Roberts's rampage in agonizing and sensational detail. In spite of that, another part of the story quickly emerged that couldn't be ignored.

Most people would react to such an atrocity in their communities with vehement anger and vengeance—at least at first. But the Amish people of Nickel Mines chose to walk a different path. A journalist wrote an insightful article entitled, "What the Amish Are Teaching America":

> The evening of the shooting, Amish neighbors from the Nickel Mines community gathered to process their grief with each other and mental health counselors.... But one question they asked might surprise us outsiders. What, they wondered, can we do to help the family of the shooter? Plans were already underway for a horse-and-buggy caravan to visit Charles Carl Roberts' family with offers of food and condolences. The Amish, it seems, don't automatically translate their grieving into revenge. Rather, they believe in redemption.[10]

The parents, relatives, and community members who gathered that night were not superhuman. They felt the shock and pain of their loss as deeply as any of us would. Unlike Charles, however, they didn't blame God or shake their fists at heaven, demanding to know why this had happened.

They refused to pick up stones for a stoning. Instead, they relied on God's love for strength.

They trusted in God's ability to use their pain for a higher purpose. That was enough to stop bitterness in its tracks. The people who had lost the most heard God's voice through the "megaphone of pain," and their subsequent actions became a powerful example of God's grace, love, and redemption for all to see.

The Amish community glittered brilliantly like a diamond, reflecting the God of all grace. When we realize God is not to blame for our suffering and when we trust His purposes for the pain in our lives, we too will shine.

Diamonds in the Rough

Diamonds—the hardest known natural substance in the world—are considered by many the most prized of possessions because of their brilliant shine. Famous for dispersing radiant sparkles of light, they have adorned kings and queens alike in spite of their crude origin.

Diamonds are wrought from carbon-based deposits embedded miles beneath the earth's surface. It takes years of intense *pressure* and *high temperatures* for carbon to be transformed into a beautiful diamond.

As for you, the Master Jeweler preplanned how He would use the *heat* and *pressure of injustice* in your life. But rough, rugged rocks of resentment, deeply embedded in your heart, can interfere with God's handiwork and stall the transformation process.

As you dig deep to remove those rocks and hand them to the Redeemer, He will cut and craft them into dazzling diamonds. They then become a shining testimony of His purpose through pain—no longer do they remain diamonds in the rough.

BURIED UNDER ROCKS OF REGRET

When the Person You Need to Forgive Is You

IT'S EXHAUSTING...LIKE CARRYING around a brick-laden backpack wherever we go. The extra weight makes hard work out of everything we do.

The Mission, an Academy-Award-winning film, is the true story of Rodrigo Mendoza, a man whose guilt becomes so great he decides to carry his burden—literally.

A mercenary and slave trader in eighteenth-century Brazil, Mendoza ruthlessly hunts native people as if they were animals and sells them to plantation owners. For him, the promise of gold justifies the cruelty. The moment we see him, his eyes convey a cold and remorseless heart.

While on a lengthy expedition capturing slaves, the woman he loves falls for another man—his brother, Felipe. Upon hearing the news, Mendoza kills him in a jealous rage. Because the fight was a duel of honor, he is immune from the law. Yet even he knows God's law offers no such protection.

Strongly stricken with guilt for all his offenses, Mendoza retreats to a Jesuit monastery, turning his tiny room into a self-imposed prison. There he intends to spend the rest of his life in a penance of pain and isolation.

Enter Father Gabriel, a Jesuit priest whose work is to build a mission among the remote Guarani Indians, the very tribe Mendoza had attacked in repeated slave raids. When Gabriel hears of Mendoza's extreme remorse, he sees an opportunity to redeem a life gone wrong. He urges Mendoza to return to the jungle, this time to help the Indians he once hunted. He tells him there *is* a way out.

Mendoza rejects the very idea of redemption, saying no penance could be hard enough. Gabriel doesn't argue whether or not there is penance "hard enough" to cleanse Mendoza's conscience. He knows very well there isn't—only the grace of God can do that. But he senses if Mendoza will try it, God will find a way past his guilt to the place of freedom. Gabriel tells Mendoza his quest is a "burden of freedom."

Their laborious journey to the mission is arduous and dangerous. Dense jungle, steep cliffs, and thundering waterfalls are all obstacles on Mendoza's road to redemption. To "pay" for his sins, he must drag behind him a symbol of the weight of his enormous guilt: a bag filled with 100 pounds of Spanish armor. No matter how many times he falls or how far back he slides through the mud, he stubbornly gets up again, never letting go of his burden.

They finally arrive at the mission. The Indians are excited to see Gabriel and begin to welcome him.

Then they see Mendoza, covered in mud and pulling the bag of armor behind him. Clearly, he no longer poses a threat to them. Exhausted from the journey and the weight of his burden—both internal and external—he falls to his knees before them. Through the years he has stolen their young, scattered their families, and robbed them of peace and security. They have many reasons to hate him.

An Indian man grabs a knife and holds it to Mendoza's throat. The former slave trader doesn't flinch. He is prepared to accept the punishment he deserves. One of the priests moves to intervene, but Gabriel stops him. He knows Mendoza's moment of truth has arrived.

Then, in a vivid portrayal of God's grace, the man takes the knife from Mendoza's throat and uses it to cut the thick strands of rope binding him to his burden of "sin." The Indian kicks the bag over the edge of a high, steep cliff, and everyone watches it fall and ultimately crash to the bottom of a deep ravine far below them.

Mendoza begins to sob uncontrollably, finally releasing a flood of pent-up emotion. The Indians gather around him and comfortingly stroke his head as he weeps.

This moving scene is analogous to the freedom from guilt we have when Jesus removes the heavy bag of sin from our backs and throws it far away from us "into the depths of the sea,"[1] never to be seen again.

Good-bye, guilt. Good-bye, regret. Good riddance. Gone forever.

As Paul wrote, "There is now no condemnation for those who are in Christ Jesus."[2] We might think of this as the "no condemnation" clause in our new covenant with God, made possible only by the shed blood of Christ. We are forgiven of all past offenses and even all future ones—we are *totally free*, just like Mendoza was when the thick strands of rope were slashed and he was literally released from his weighty burden.

But as Gabriel said to Mendoza, God also gives us the "burden of freedom." That means this incomparable gift is ours only if we *accept it* and thereby assume the responsibilities that go with it. Mendoza was free to refuse. He could have rejected the grace extended to him and climbed down the ravine to take up his penance again.

I have, in fact, counseled many people who have done that. They were determined to hang on to their guilt. Surprisingly, forgiving ourselves is not always easy to do. In fact, sometimes it is more difficult than forgiving others. We must learn to forgive ourselves, even if we don't feel like it or feel worthy of it. We must crawl out from under the crushing rocks of regret.

How Do We Get Over Guilt?

Over the years, I've developed the *Biblical Counseling Library* on over 100 different topics. One is on learning how to deal positively and effectively with our guilt, and allowing God to fully apply the completed work of redemption He accomplished at Calvary. Consider the powerful acrostic F-O-R-G-I-V-E-N:

Find the source of your guilt

Rodrigo Mendoza knew exactly where his guilt came from. He was tormented by memories of past actions he knew were wrong. This is *true guilt*.

As strange as it may sound, true guilt is our friend and occurs only because of what we have done. Just as a fever is a signal to our bodies that something is not right, true guilt is a spiritual warning. It tells us our sins are veiling who we are, *children of God*, and what we're called to do, *reflect His image*.

> False guilt causes a deep sense of unworthiness—completely opposite of how God sees us.

There also is *false guilt*, based not on specific sinful actions, but on being ashamed of who we are. False guilt comes from perceiving ourselves as basically defective. It surfaces when we can't stop blaming ourselves, even though we have done nothing wrong or we have long since confessed and turned from our sin. Such unfounded shame causes a deep sense of unworthiness—completely opposite of how God sees us.

In the seventeenth century, Bishop Robert South said, "Guilt upon the conscience, like rust upon iron, both defiles and consumes it, gnawing and creeping into it, as that does which at last eats out the very heart and substance of the metal."[3]

That kind of toxic guilt is your enemy and certainly not the will of God. His purpose for guilt is to correct you and build you up, not destroy your heart and cripple your soul and spirit. The Bible says, "Godly sorrow brings repentance that leads to salvation and leaves no regret, but worldly sorrow brings death."[4]

When you struggle with feelings of guilt, begin by discerning the difference between friend and foe. Acknowledge your sins honestly, but reject the temptation to see yourself as fundamentally flawed and unworthy.

Dig out from under that rock pile of regret!

Own responsibility for your sin

Once you know the source of your guilt, the next step is to own up to it: Repent and confess the offense. Johann Christoph Arnold wrote:

> Guilt works in secret, and it loses its power only when it is allowed out into the open. Often our desire to appear righteous keeps us from admitting our wrongs. Why acknowledge a foolish choice or a dumb mistake? Yet the more we try to push such things to the back of our minds, the more they will plague us, even if subconsciously. Eventually guilt will add to guilt, and we will become cramped and weighed down.[5]

To repent means to change your mind—to agree with God that you have sinned. When you do, God's response is guaranteed: "If we confess our sins, he is faithful and just and will forgive us our sins and purify us from all unrighteousness."[6]

Then why do feelings of guilt sometimes persist even after you have confessed your sin to God and accepted His forgiveness? It could be that you also need to repair the damage your offense has caused. Until then, you cannot be completely free.

Jesus said, "If you are offering your gift at the altar and there remember that your brother has something against you, leave your gift there in front of the altar. First go and be reconciled to your brother; then come and offer your gift."[7] Confess your sins. Then repay those whom you've harmed. When you do, you'll rob your guilt of power and purpose—it will die like fire without fuel.

Repentance and restitution will keep those rocks of regret from piling up!

Realize that God means what He says

Before Mendoza and the priests reached the mission where the Indian freed him permanently of his burden, one of the brothers couldn't bear to watch his suffering any longer. He cut the bag of armor, and it fell to the bottom of one of the cliffs they had just climbed. Without a word, Mendoza went back down and retrieved it. Later, the priest who cut off the bag approached Father Gabriel for support. Gabriel replies that until Mendoza thinks his penance has been sufficient, no one will be able to convince him otherwise.

God's forgiveness is free—*and enough.* It can't be purchased with any amount of penance. The Bible says, "In him we have redemption through his blood, the forgiveness of sins, in accordance with the riches of God's grace that he lavished on us with all wisdom and understanding."[8]

Free enough... but that doesn't mean it is always accepted.

How many times have we heard the phrase, "If it sounds too good to be true, it probably is"? By the time we reach adulthood, we've been suckered one too many times by false hope and are deeply suspicious of any claims that promise us something for nothing.

But God is not another smooth talker. There are no hidden clauses in the contract. Forgiveness delivers the goods exactly as advertised: complete, unconditional, and absolutely free. When you suffer from prolonged guilt, that is a sign you have not yet learned to take God at His word.

Choose to believe what God says. *Thank Him* for the gift of His Son, who paid for your forgiveness. Do both, even if you don't feel forgiven. And then refuse to harbor any more accusatory thoughts. Refuse to be tempted to tote around a few rocks of regret as penance.

Give up dwelling on the past

Mendoza needn't have carried a single ounce of armor through the jungle, much less 100 pounds. To God, his penance was an unnecessary gesture. Why? Because Jesus had already carried it for him. Payment had been made in full.

Ashley called me one evening at *Hope in the Night* because Brian, a Christian man who was head-over-heels in love with her, asked her to marry him. It didn't take much to hear the hesitation in her voice.

"So what's the problem?" I asked.

"The problem is I can't say yes. I don't deserve him."

Ashley had been married once before, and the relationship came to a sudden end when she had an affair with another man.

"It was stupid and completely wrong. I will never be able to forgive myself for how badly I hurt my first husband. I can't marry Brian because of my past failures."

> If you cling to the past and refuse to forgive yourself, you "play God" with your guilt and claim the right to undo what He has done.

Sometimes what we need to hear is the last thing we expect to hear.

"Ashley, do you think you are smarter than God?"

Of course I was not trying to accuse her, but only to help her see an important truth. Although some sins—such as adultery—bring more severe consequences than others, to God, sin is sin. He forgave *all* our sins—every last one. The sweeping scope of grace makes some hearts soar, and others stumble. It just seems too good to be true. Yes, it is too good, but *it is true.*

If you cling to the past and refuse to forgive yourself, you "play God" with your guilt and claim the right to undo what He has done. The very last words Jesus spoke on the cross were, "It is finished."[9]

That means there's nothing left to do. No bags left to drag through the jungle. No bags of rocks to weigh your heart down. No rock piles of regret to crush your spirits. Sometimes we all need to be reminded, "This means you!"

Happily, Ashley listened and began to forgive herself. Without her bag of guilt, she was free to give up the past and enjoy the present.

Invest time in renewing your mind

Being free from the past means you can now exercise the phenomenal power that is yours in each new moment: the power to choose what you think and what you believe.

Think about it. The only time you have is this moment now. The past, in which you are investing so much energy feeling guilty, is gone. Nothing you do or say now will change what has already occurred. The future, about which you worry so much, is also out of your reach—and always will be.

Any influence you have over the course of your life can only be exercised in the present tense. Here and now your mind and thoughts belong to you and will obey your intentions. The Bible says, "Put off your old self, which is being corrupted by its deceitful desires; to be made new in the attitude of your minds."[10]

Put off your old way of thinking about your guilt. To forgive yourself, take time to actively affirm what you know to be true about God's grace. Read, memorize, and let your thoughts dwell on scriptures that emphasize the forgiveness of God and the grace He has extended to you in Christ Jesus. Make a habit of thanking and praising Him every day for His gift to you of guilt-free living, and for freeing you from ever having to spend another moment under that stony mound of regret.

Verify truth when Satan accuses

Take hold of truth, because Satan *will* accuse you. You can count on it. That's his favorite weapon.

After Jesus was baptized, the Spirit led Him into the wilderness. There, Satan challenged and tempted the Son of God. "If You really are the Son of God, You'd be able to feed yourself. If You really are

Precious Stones against a Black Background

The **opal** is prized for its array of colors inside a single stone—transparent pools of blue, gray, and yellow, translucent swirls of aqua, white, and pink. The Latin word *opalus* means "precious stone." While this gem is fascinating, it is also fragile—susceptible to dehydration and cracking. Overall, the opal is characterized as *weak*.

When you have personally compromised your convictions—when you feel buried under rocks of regret—and your conscience is gouged by guilt, in no way do you feel precious to God. Like the opal's physical characteristics, you feel fundamentally weak.

You may feel unworthy to be loved...unable to forgive yourself...unfit to embrace God's grace. But it is God's will that you forgive yourself as freely as He forgives you.

When you give yourself to the Lord, He gives you His grace—His unfailing forgiveness, unearned compassion, unmerited mercy. And this wide array of blessing is placed against the blackness of your past. As any jeweler knows, the opal's beauty is best displayed when placed on a dark background. When you release your painful rocks to the Master Polisher, a black background will make you shine even brighter.

the Son of God, His angels would save You if You threw Yourself off this cliff."[11]

How much more should you expect to endure Satan's accusations, especially since you know you have sinned?

"If you really were a child of God, how could you have done such a thing? Get back under that rock pile where you belong."

Fortunately, Jesus modeled how to counter Satan, whom He calls the "father of lies."[12] He wielded a weapon—the Word of God— the *truth*. Three powerful words—"It is written"—set Satan on his way.

Each time Satan tempted Jesus to prove Himself, Jesus answered with the Word of God. You must do the same when you are tempted to believe that God's forgiveness doesn't apply to you—that rocks of regret will weigh you down for life.

It is written: "He has not dealt with us according to our sins, nor punished us according to our iniquities. For as the heavens are high above the earth, so great is His mercy toward those who fear Him; as far as the east is from the west, so far has He removed our transgressions from us."[13]

Truth is your most powerful weapon. Pick it up *and use it.*

Exchange your life for the life of Christ

When Lucy was arrested for drug trafficking, she had no one to call for help but her parents. She came from a Christian family, but after college had wandered far from what she knew to be true.

"Sitting in that jail cell was bad enough," she said. "But I thought I would die from the pain I saw on Daddy's face when he came to pick me up."

> God will never direct you to crawl back under a rock pile of regret.

In time, Lucy's parents forgave her and were ready to forget the whole episode. But she continued to feel ashamed and worthless.

"I don't think I can forgive myself for the stupid things I've done."

"Of course you can't," I said. This is not what she thought she'd hear when she called me.

"Well, not without help, anyway," I continued.

The truth is, none of us can live the Christian life in our own strength. We must realize that Christ not only became a substitute for us in His death, but stands in for us in *life* as well. Having purchased our forgiveness, He then transforms us inside out so we are able to receive forgiveness. We can personally claim Galatians 2:20: "I have been crucified with Christ and I no longer live, but Christ lives in me. The life I live in the body, I live by faith in the Son of God, who loved me and gave himself for me."

There is no better news than that!

And what's your part? To let go of your life in exchange for living in the power of His. You are to let Him live through you. And He will never direct you to crawl back under a rock pile of regret.

Notice that God brings your feelings in line with the facts when you obey Him

There were no spiritual "facts" driving Rodrigo Mendoza to drag 100 pounds of armor through the jungle. He was compelled by only one thing: his *feelings* of shame and unworthiness. Having murdered his brother and enslaved hundreds of innocent natives, he felt ineligible for any measure of grace.

And yet he followed Father Gabriel to the mission. Certain that his attempt at penance would fail, he did it anyway, suffering every step of the way. What he didn't realize was his feelings were irrelevant. He walked right into a "trap" laid by the Master of second chances.

When the Indian's knife cut away Mendoza's burden of guilt, the *fact* of God's unconditional forgiveness suddenly became clear. His old feelings of unworthiness and self-condemnation fell to the bottom of the ravine. Then grace replaced them with profound gratitude and acceptance of God's free gift—the gift of forgiveness.

Perseverance in spite of what you feel pays off. Forgiving others and forgiving yourself—even when you don't feel like it—guarantees freedom. Surely the writer of the book of Hebrews understood this, for he wrote, "You have need of endurance, so that when you have done the will of God you may receive what is promised."[14]

The will of God is that you forgive yourself as freely as He forgives you. That is the essence of the good news of Jesus Christ. That is the "no condemnation" clause that releases you from the punishment for your failures.[15]

Redemption Is Yours

Nowhere in the Bible will you find a list of sins that are exempted from God's grace. That means no matter what you've done or how unforgivable you feel, as a Christian, redemption is already yours.

You are F-O-R-G-I-V-E-N. Period. No exceptions, not even for you. But remember to do your part—confessing your sins to God and others, and repairing any damage you've done. Then let God do His part—freeing you and empowering you to become all He intends you to be.

13

The Power of the Empty Bag

Fringe Benefits of Forgiveness

After presenting a seminar on the remarkable power of forgiveness, I was pleased to see one of the participants walking toward me. I had noticed her listening attentively, her face standing out in the crowd because her countenance was radiant.

When Beverly's husband died in a motorcycle accident years ago, she was left on her own to raise her daughter, Meagan. The family had recently moved to a new city where Beverly had no friends or relatives. To make matters worse, her husband left their finances in a mess. Beverly suddenly had to work two jobs just to survive.

"In the first few days after Barry's accident, I felt like I was standing at the edge of a cliff. I was depressed and distraught. I thought about how easy it would be to just let myself fall and never come back. That's what I would have done if Meagan had not been in my life."

Beverly found the strength to go on by caring for her daughter. Together, they weathered their grief and rebuilt their lives.

Then one day, several years later, Meagan was late returning from the mall with some friends. The phone rang.

"I don't know why, but I knew as soon as I heard the phone that something was wrong," Beverly recalled.

Something *was* wrong—tragically wrong. A drunk driver had

run a red light and crashed into the car carrying the girls. Meagan and one of her friends were killed. Two more were hospitalized.

"I learned the meaning of total darkness that day. It fell on me like a thousand heavy black curtains."

The depression Beverly had battled when her husband died now overpowered her without a fight. Having lost Meagan, she felt she had no reason to live.

Dense boulders plunged into her bag with such force that she collapsed emotionally. "I started drinking a lot. I had to do something to drown the hatred I felt for the drunk driver. My rage was unbearable."

One night, drunk and barely able to stand up, Beverly left a lounge not far from her house and got behind the wheel of her car to drive home. She doesn't remember the trip at all. The next morning, she woke up in her car, parked in her front yard, inches away from crashing into the house.

"I wept so hard," she told me, tears returning to her eyes as she spoke. "I cried and cried. I cried for Meagan and out of shame for myself. I was horrified that—being so drunk—I could have killed someone else's child. I was horrified that I had done exactly what the man did who took Meagan from me. My heart broke, and for the first time in years, I called out to God."

Beverly begged Him to help her...and to forgive her.

"I told God I'd do anything, if only He'd save me from this horrible grief. I didn't hear a voice or anything, but something remarkable happened. Though my tears kept coming, I suddenly realized I wasn't crying for myself anymore, or for Meagan. I was weeping for the drunk driver who had killed her. His name was Sam. For the first time, I could identify with him. For the first time, I felt pain for *him*. I knew right then what I had to do. I had to forgive Sam."

That proved to be a challenge, but over the next several months Beverly quit drinking. She learned that forgiving Sam did not depend on what she felt. It was a choice. When she was ready, she finally wrote to him in prison.

"It was a short letter. I shared with him what I experienced that morning in my car, and the compassion I felt for him. I shared that God also has compassion for him and that God loves him deeply. I forgave him and said *whatever debt he still owed for his actions, it wasn't to me.*"

> There is no heart forgiveness cannot mend, no hurt it cannot heal, no sin it cannot cleanse, and no life it cannot change.

It was obvious that in dismissing Sam's debt, Beverly really freed herself. Her emotional bag, which had been ready to burst, had been emptied—totally flattened. The woman who stood before me bore no resemblance to the grief-stricken, suicidal, purposeless victim in her story. She had been utterly transformed by the amazing power of forgiveness. Like hard, sharp fragments of flint shaped into arrowheads and made into useful tools, the immense energy behind Beverly's anger had been redirected and reshaped into a positive instrument in the Lord's hands.

The Power of Forgiveness

God created Beverly, like each of us, with three inner needs—needs for love, significance, and security. Only He can completely satisfy those needs. Beverly first tried to meet these needs illegitimately—through her daughter, through drinking, and even through withholding forgiveness in order to achieve a false sense of significance.

Finally realizing her own inability to fully satisfy her needs, Beverly wisely accepted God's perfect provision and discovered, along with it, the perfect peace that had eluded her for so long. Beverly learned firsthand the truth of Philippians 4:19: "My God will meet all your needs according to his glorious riches in Christ Jesus."

Discover the Treasure Inside

Geodes are magnificent crystals that can form inside any cavity beneath the earth's surface. Over time, a slow, steady dripping of minerals deposited inside one of these cavities becomes a sea of sparkling quartz, while the exterior simply looks like a dull, rough rock. The outside of the geode bears no resemblance to the inside, and gives no hint of the beauty that lies within.

When you harbor unforgiveness within you, it's like shutting out the dripping of minerals that can create beautiful quartz crystals. But when you release your unforgiveness to God and begin to pray for your offender, an amazing transformation occurs—God begins to produce shining character traits within you.

One prayer at a time, and one prayer after another, is like a steady deposit of minerals inside a cavity within the ground. Through prayer, God softens your spirit and calms your heart to make you as beautiful on the inside as the sea of quartz inside a geode.

Be encouraged. What may not initially be seen on the outside one day will be evident to all. Like a rock cutter who opens a geode to reveal the beauty within, so is the Master Lapidarian, who will reveal the inner beauty of your Christlike character to those around you and to a world that needs to be caught up in its wonder.

Forgiveness is powerful, purposeful, and pervasive. There is no heart it cannot mend, no hurt it cannot heal, no sin it cannot cleanse, and no life it cannot change. It dislodges and displaces the biggest of boulders, saving many from the brink of disaster. Stories like Beverly's could fill thousands of books and we still would not have exhausted the many reasons to practice the remarkable power of forgiveness.

The Benefits of Forgiveness

The blessings that accompany forgiveness go on and on. Joy is renewed, relationships are restored, hopefulness is reclaimed, and energy is revitalized. Let's look at some additional benefits you experience when you forgive.

Forgiveness Leads to Better Health

I am often amazed at how many Christians still liken forgiveness to a dose of bad-tasting medicine. It's as if they see God standing over them with a bottle of castor oil in one hand and a spoon the size of a mixing bowl in the other. "This is going to be unpleasant," they imagine Him saying sternly. "Open up."

With that kind of imagery, who can blame them for pursing their lips and stubbornly resisting forgiveness?

But forgiveness is not a dose of unpleasant medicine, not a cross to bear. Forgiveness is a perfect prescription for wellness from the Great Physician Himself. It is an antidote for poisonous thoughts and emotions, yes, but forgiveness is also good for your physical health.

"I know it sounds strange, but I think my heart attack saved my life," Max told me one evening when he called *Hope in the Night*. "For years, I thought that by refusing to forgive my father I was getting back at him for everything he had done to me. I was wrong."

Max's father was an alcoholic who routinely heaped verbal abuse onto his mother and him. He added insult to injury by engaging in a series of flagrant affairs with other women in the community. Max vowed never to forget his mother's humiliation or his own pain.

There was no way Max was willing to remove even the smallest stone from his burlap bag. Even after his father quit drinking and started working to salvage his marriage, Max held on to his bitterness more tightly than ever. It was as though Max had a stranglehold on the neck of his bag (see Appendix E on page 206).

To friends, Max described himself as "handicapped" by his "toxic" childhood. As an adult, he often had a headache he couldn't shake and mysterious stomach pains that doctors couldn't diagnose.

It was not uncommon for him to come down with a nasty case of the flu after visiting his parents for a few days.

"I wanted to make *him* pay," Max told me, "but it turns out I was the one paying. I found out the hard way that unforgiveness is costly."

At age 42, Max suffered a serious heart attack. Doctors were baffled, and Max was rattled enough to finally listen to the message his body had been sending him for years. He entered counseling and began the work of forgiving his father. It was then he realized the toll unforgiveness had taken on his health.

Dr. Guy Pettit, a writer and lecturer from New Zealand, sums up the link between forgiveness and health:

> Unforgiveness...can have profound effects on the way your body functions. Muscles tighten, causing imbalances or pain in your neck, back and limbs. Blood flow to the joint surfaces is decreased, making it more difficult for the blood to remove wastes from the tissues and reducing the supply of oxygen and nutrients to the cells. Normal processes of repair and recovery from injury or arthritis are impaired. Clenching of the jaws contributes to problems with teeth and jaw joints. Headaches are probable. Chronic pain may be worsened.
>
> The list goes on: blood flow to the heart is constricted. Digestion is impaired. Breathing is restricted. The immune system functions less well, increasing vulnerability to infections and perhaps malignancy. Injuries and accidents through inattention are more likely.[1]

Not a pretty picture. More than 1,000 studies published over the past decade support these findings. Unforgiveness produces a toxic biochemical brew in the human body that takes a measurable toll on your health.

Brenda Goodman wrote in *Psychology Today*:

> If physical exercise had a mental equivalent, it would probably be the process of forgiveness. Researchers continue

to tally the benefits of burying the hatchet—lower blood pressure and heart rate, less depression, a better immune system and a longer life, among others.[2]

Modern science is reinforcing what our Creator has plainly told us all along: *Forgiveness is good for you.* God insists that you let go of the anger and resentment you feel against those who harm you—not to let your offenders off the hook, but to move them from your hook to God's hook, freeing you of the weight of carrying them and the pain they've caused you. Forgiveness helps you emerge from difficult experiences with your health intact and enables you to seize God's gift of abundant life, which is brimming with possibility.

> Energy spent on anger is energy lost. Forgiveness reclaims our energy and redirects it.

Carrying boulder-filled bags around is really rough on your body!

Forgiveness Brings Improved Potential

Forgiveness has the power to set you free. Forgiveness releases your grasp from the burlap bag that burdens you so you can run the race of life as God intended. Bitterness, anger, and revenge are prisons you can escape at any time once you realize forgiveness is the key that opens the door.

But leaving these dark crippling cells is only half the value of freedom. When you emerge into the sunlight again, you are free from the chains that held you, the burlap bag that weighed you down. Even better, you are free to pursue your life with renewed passion and purpose. Energy spent on anger and revenge is energy lost. Forgiveness reclaims that energy and redirects it to make your life better than ever.

Raul was a promising young journalist. He had worked hard to land a job at a prestigious national magazine. For the first few weeks, the job went well. His work was noticed right away by senior editors, who hinted he had a bright future with the publication.

Then trouble started. Apparently jealous of his early success, Raul's supervisor began making life hard for him. She assigned the most promising stories to other writers, sent Raul on wild goose chases, and even altered some of his submissions—for the worse.

"I would go home fuming every night," Raul told me. "Barely a day went by without another one of Monica's conniving deeds or outright attacks."

Even so, Raul did his best to keep the situation in perspective. As a Christian, he knew God's commandment to forgive, and even to love his enemies. However, one day, Monica went too far. She took an idea Raul spent weeks developing and passed it off as her own. The story was a big success, and she took all the credit.

Over the next few weeks, the quality of Raul's work declined steadily. He developed an attitude that was hard to miss. In short, the promise he showed at first was starting to look bleaker by the day.

"I was spending all my time either trying to evade her dirty tricks or plotting my revenge. I was bitter. I knew better, but it didn't matter. I would have paid a lot just to get back at her."

In the end, he almost *did* pay a lot. It nearly cost him his job. When the time came for his performance review, senior staffers made it clear he had only one chance left. They gave him an ultimatum: Shape up or ship out!

"I was devastated, but I also knew they were right. God spoke through them to remind me what I already knew. If I didn't figure out how to forgive Monica, somebody was going down—and it probably wasn't her."

Raul realized in time that unforgiveness was sapping the potential he had worked so hard to develop. The energy he poured into fantasizing about his revenge was wasted energy, and his work suffered as a result. It wasn't easy, but it was as clear as crystal what he needed to do.

Raul eventually forgave Monica, and even decided to do something kind for her every day. Soon his excitement at work returned, and he was writing better than ever.

"I wish I could say Monica had a change of heart. But by forgiving her, I had a change of heart—I got myself back."

When God commands you to forgive, it is with your good in mind. He knows when you let go of bitterness and revenge, when you bid farewell to the rocks and boulders, there is no limit to what He can accomplish in you and through you.

Forgiveness Leads to Greater Christlikeness

When the Spirit of Christ is rooted within you, He produces spiritual fruit—you are increasingly conformed to the character of Christ. (The moment you entrust your life to Jesus, you are "sealed" with the Holy Spirit, who lives within you for the rest of your life.) [3] Therefore, the next time you are wronged, allow the Spirit of Christ to produce His fruit in you—the fruit of a forgiving heart, which includes love, joy, peace, patience, kindness, goodness, faithfulness, gentleness, and self-control.[4]

Love—You refuse to keep a record of the wrongs people have committed against you. "Above all, love each other deeply, because love covers over a multitude of sins."[5]

Joy—You are joyful that because of God's goodness and His sovereignty over all events in your life—even the painful ones—He will ultimately use them for good. As the apostle Paul said while under house arrest, chained to a guard 24 hours a day, "I will continue to rejoice, for I know that through your prayers and the help given by the Spirit of Jesus Christ, what has happened to me will turn out for my deliverance."[6]

Peace—You seek to resolve any difficulty, hurt, or division, wanting the offender to be right with God. "Aim for perfection, listen to my appeal, be of one mind, live in peace. And the God of love and peace will be with you."[7]

Patience—You recognize your offender is not "fixed in cement" and could one day change. "Love is patient."[8]

Kindness—You unselfishly bless others and seek to meet their needs through thoughtful words and deeds. "Render true judgments, show kindness and mercy to one another."[9]

Goodness—You hold to moral principles and purity even in the midst of controversy. "Live such good lives among the pagans that, though they accuse you of doing wrong, they may see your good deeds and glorify God."[10]

Faithfulness—You faithfully pray that the one who has caused you pain will one day have a changed life. "Be joyful in hope, patient in affliction, faithful in prayer."[11]

Gentleness—You respond to the anger of others with a calm gentleness. "A gentle answer turns away wrath, but a harsh word stirs up anger."[12]

Self-control—You decide ahead of time how to respond to a difficult person when conflict arises. "Prepare your minds for action; be self-controlled."[13]

Forgiveness Points Others to God

Author Lee Strobel tells the story of an eight-year-old girl caught shoplifting a book. Her parents brought her to Lee's office. The girl tearfully admitted she took the book, knowing it was wrong.

Lee suggested as punishment she should pay the price of the book—$5—plus three times that. The girl nodded sadly, but it was obvious that $20 seemed a huge amount of money to her.

Seizing the opportunity to teach her something about Jesus, Lee then reached into his desk drawer and pulled out his personal checkbook. He wrote out a check for $20 from his own account and held it out to her for the girl to see. Her mouth dropped open.

"I'm going to pay your penalty so you don't have to," he told her. "Do you know why I would do that?"

Bewildered, she shook her head.

He continued, "Because I love you. Because I care about you. Because you are valuable to me. And please remember this: That's how Jesus feels about you, too. Except even more."

The girl took the gift and "a look of absolute relief and joy blossomed on her face." To her, forgiveness would never again be "theoretical." She had experienced it for herself.[14]

Forgiveness Brings Change to the World

True forgiveness always begins in the privacy of a wounded heart as unseen yieldedness to God. From there it may grow into a quiet, one-on-one encounter between the offended and the offender. But sometimes that's just the beginning. The smallest act of forgiveness radiates outward, like ripples in a pond, and can change the destructive course of families, churches, communities, and even whole societies.

Who knows how often your world hangs in the balance, waiting for you to choose between revenge and forgiveness? Empty bags are powerful...penetrating hearts, changing minds, and transforming lives (see Appendix C on page 201).

> Genuine forgiveness has the power to transform the heart and conscience of your world.

In February 1965, eight days after being beaten and shot in the stomach by a police officer, Jimmie Lee Jackson died quietly in a Selma, Alabama hospital. His crime? He had tackled a state trooper who was mercilessly beating his mother as police broke up a voter registration rally for black people at a local church.

For many civil rights proponents, Jackson's death was the last straw. They wondered whether nonviolence and forgiveness—the cornerstones of the civil rights movement up to that point—were hopelessly naïve strategies when pitted against such a determined and violent adversary. Maybe it was time to meet force with force, they argued.

But Martin Luther King Jr., already a leader of the movement, knew that forgiveness was far more than a political strategy. As a Christian, he understood that forgiveness has the unique power to put an end to injustice and change the world. He knew a bag empty of animosity, anger, and angst actually carried monumental weight. In his book *Strength to Love,* King wrote,

> We must develop and maintain the capacity to forgive. Whoever is devoid of the power to forgive is devoid of the power to love....
>
> To our most bitter opponents we say: We shall match your capacity to inflict suffering by your capacity to endure suffering. We shall meet your physical force with soul force. Do to us what you will, and we shall continue to love you....
>
> Throw us in jail, and we shall still love you. Send your hooded perpetrators of violence into your community at the midnight hour and beat us and leave us half dead, and we shall still love you. But be ye assured that we will wear you down by our capacity to suffer.
>
> One day we shall win our freedom, but not only for ourselves. We shall so appeal to your heart and conscience that we shall win you in the process, and our victory will be a double victory.[15]

The "soul force" King spoke of had dramatic results. Genuine forgiveness has the power to transform the heart and conscience of society. He understood the necessity of extending forgiveness...even if he and his fellow advocates didn't feel like doing so. In forgiving, Dr. King said, we lay down our own lives so that God's love and mercy can replace fear and hatred, transforming our enemies into friends and allies in the process.

This remarkable idea is not new, of course. Jesus modeled it two millennia earlier on the cross. Paul told the Romans, "When we were still powerless, Christ died for the ungodly. Very rarely will anyone die for a righteous man, though for a good man someone might possibly dare to die. But God demonstrates his own love for us in this: While we were still sinners, Christ died for us."[16]

Three weeks after Jimmie Lee's death, 600 people set out to march peacefully from Selma to Montgomery to plead their case to Governor George Wallace. The people made it only six blocks from where they started. In full view of reporters and television cameras, police attacked the marchers with clubs, tear gas, and whips and drove them back.

Six hundred burlap bags could have been filled in one day over that one atrocity.

At the head of the march, John Lewis, who later became a U.S. Congressman, took the first blows. Years later, he explained his Christian commitment to nonviolence and forgiveness: "If you believe there is a spark of the divine in every human being, you cannot get to the point where you hate that person, or despise that person...even if that person beats you.... You have to have the capacity, the ability to forgive."[17]

Lewis knew forgiveness may start as a gift from one person to another, but once given, nothing can contain it. Forgiveness changes *hearts*, not just laws, and can knock over stone walls of strife like dominoes. After what happened in Selma that day, people all across America felt grief and shame at what they saw in the newspapers and on television. Hearts *did* change, and America did become a better place.

Two weeks later, the marchers tried again. Their number had grown from 600 to 25,000, and this time they reached Montgomery. Despite all they had been through, there were no begrudging, bent-over figures dragging bags of bitterness on that march. Just five months after that, President Johnson signed into law the Voting Rights Act of 1965.

All those working for nonviolent change chose to do it "God's way." They forgave their enemies one person and one act of violence at a time, and the impact of their choice did not stop there. It changed the world.

Empty bags get people's attention.

≈

The Result of Forgiveness

Beverly was forever changed by her decision to forgive. But I was delighted to learn, as I listened to her that night, she was not yet finished with her story. By writing Sam a letter dismissing his debt to her, she did all she had set out to do.

She did not expect what happened next.

Sam wrote back. He told her the guilt he felt every waking moment since the incident had nearly crushed him. He attempted suicide in prison. He hadn't dared to ask God to forgive him because he was sure he didn't deserve it.

Her letter changed that.

"My two little paragraphs were enough to cause Sam to fall on his knees and repent. He became a Christian. Since then, he's shared my letter with anyone who will listen."

Now I knew why Beverly's face beamed so brightly. After her terrible loss, forgiveness rescued her from the bondage of depression and bitterness. But it didn't stop there. Her decision to forgive continues to transform the lives of people she's never even met.

Empty bags *do* get people's attention!

14

A Heart of Stone Finds Hope and Healing

Asking Forgiveness, Finding Freedom

WHENEVER I HEAR THE WORD *forgiveness*, my immediate thought goes to my father—not because of my success at forgiveness, but because of my failure. I didn't forgive him for a number of years. I didn't feel like doing that.

My first major problem was in seeing no reason to forgive my father. My second major problem was seeing no reason to ask my father to forgive me. My logical, math-oriented mind reasoned: *Why forgive someone who hasn't changed?* It just didn't add up. He had not changed, nor had he seen any reason to change.

My father had a heart of stone—stone that seemed impenetrable.

As for me, I focused only on his faults. My grievances were many because, in my view, his faults were many. He acted arrogantly, as though he was a god unto himself. He often seemed condescending—belittling, degrading, looking down on others. His attitudes and actions were wounding, and the greatest grievance of all was the way he crushed Mother's spirit.

Many times I remember silently pleading, *You can hurt me, but please, I beg you, don't hurt her!* However, my mental pleadings were of no avail.

This was a dark time in my life. I call it my "black filter" era. (A black filter placed on a camera lens turns a daytime scene into a

185

nighttime photograph.) In truth, I looked at my father through a black filter: I had a dark view of everything he did. I didn't want to acknowledge anything good in him. After all, he was 100 percent wrong and I was 100 percent right. At least that's how I saw it.

A Challenge to Extend Forgiveness

One day during a discussion with a new acquaintance, this woman challenged me to consider my attitude: "I don't think you've ever forgiven your father." How could she say that? She didn't even know me! I felt somewhat judged by her. Defensively, I tried to explain— with humility—that Dad was the one totally in the wrong.

She again challenged, "Do you mean that you've not had a wrong attitude toward him at all?" Slowly I responded, "Well...yes...but..." I thought to myself, *Okay then, he's been 98 percent wrong, I've been only 2 percent wrong.*

To be candid, I didn't appreciate being confronted. But oh, how I needed that! I began to feel convicted. *June, even if you are only 2 percent wrong, you are still responsible before God for your 2 percent.*

The Spirit of God used the Word of God both to convict me and to compel me to action. I was surprised when I read these words spoken by Jesus: "If you are offering your gift at the altar and there remember that your brother has something against you, leave your gift there in front of the altar. First go and be reconciled to your brother; then come and offer your gift."[1]

This means God prioritizes that we have a pure heart before Him and a clear conscience in our relationships before fulfilling our responsibilities as Christians. Amazing! At that moment I knew what I needed to do: not just forgive my father, but also ask forgiveness of him.

I prayed...I planned...I prepared...and then one morning, I approached my father. He was seated at the head of the dining room table eating breakfast. Known for being eccentric, his morning meal always included the same intriguing array of items: seven almonds, one cup each of orange juice, carrot juice, and grape juice, one hard-boiled egg, one slice of homemade wheat toast, and one cup of boiled water.

Long before health foods were in fashion, my father was a health food "enthusiast," even daily resorting to eating the tiny seeds from the insides of two apricot pits. (He said the Hunza people in northern Pakistan lived to be up to 120 years old by eating the miniscule seeds; therefore, he reasoned that eating them would substantially prolong his life.)

He was reading the newspaper as I drew near.

"Dad, may I speak to you?" He peered at me above the reading glasses perched on the end of his nose. He said nothing. Still, I began my confession.

"I realize I've been an ungrateful daughter." I then proceeded to mention specific areas in which I had been ungrateful because I wanted him to know that I realized I had taken him for granted. I genuinely wanted to lighten the load in my burlap bag.

"Dad, I've never thanked you for the roof over my head, food on the table, and books for school. So, I've come to ask, 'Would you forgive me?' "

I paused, awaiting a response. Had this been a scene in a heart-warming family film, the newspaper would have fallen to the floor, my father would have sprung up from his chair (with tears in his eyes), and he would have embraced his apologetic daughter. But this was no movie. This was real life, and there wasn't an ounce of warmth in his response.

Stoically he replied, "The pleasure was all mine," as if just completing a business transaction. Immediately he returned to his newspaper. I stood there stunned and seemingly frozen in time. Seconds seemed like minutes. When I realized there would be no discussion, I quietly, awkwardly walked out of the room, numb to the weight of the invisible bag I dragged out with me. Had my bag gotten lighter through obedience to God or more loaded down by my father's cool passivity?

My father didn't change that day. But, as it turns out, something in me did. I knew I had done what was right in God's sight; therefore, I learned that Dad's response (or lack of response) should not be my impetus for what I do. I had gotten a taste of freedom!

One of the most perplexing scriptures, to me, has to be "Love your enemies."[2] When I first read this passage, I thought, *Well, that's a wonderful ideal. Of course, it's not realistic. People can't love their enemies.* However, I was wrong.

> "Love your enemies" means seeking the highest good of those who hurt you.

Initially I thought Jesus was referring to an emotional, tingly-all-over feeling kind of love (this is *eros*, meaning "passion"). Instead, the kind of love in "love your enemies" is the Greek word *agape*, which implies a commitment that seeks the highest good of another.

So what could I do in Dad's best interest? How could I seek his highest good? I pondered, *He's always misplacing his red address book. I'll locate it so that when he barks, "Where's my address book?" I'll know.*

The Master of Lapidary

He's known by many names. And although you won't find this one anywhere in Scripture, *it fits*. God is indeed the *Master of Lapidary*. He is cutting...polishing...carving...refining your unwanted rocks—making them of maximum worth.

The ancient craft of lapidary is the art of transforming rough rocks into polished stones and sparkling jewels. With consummate precision, the artisan enhances the inherent qualities of each and every stone.

Lapidarists use four main methods to create masterpieces:

- **Tumbling** involves days or weeks of continually rotating large quantities of stones with abrasives and water inside a revolving barrel (or vibrating tumbler). The lackluster stones, at the end, emerge with a smooth, mirrorlike luster.

- **Cabbing,** the earliest form of gem cutting, entails a "cabochon" cut of mostly opaque gems, such as opals, moonstones, and turquoise. A "cab" is a dome with a flat bottom and curved top.

- **Faceting,** a later form of lapidary, is the cutting of facets on transparent gems such as emeralds, rubies, and diamonds. Facets are geometric flat surfaces that act like mirrors reflecting light off each other and up through the crown of the gemstone. (The "brilliant" diamond cut, the most common style today, has either 57 or 58 facets.)

- **Carving** or **sculpting** is a trying, meticulous method of engraving a design on opaque gemstones such as coral, agate, and jade.

Just as no two rocks are identical, neither are any two people. The delight of the Master Lapidarist is to design a *unique* creation—taking the ordinary and turning it into the extraordinary, taking our trials and turning them into triumphs.

Rocks don't *feel* the effects of the lapidarist's tools, but people do. You cannot escape the pain. However, the Master's specialty is turning your pain into purpose—into meaningful purpose according to His perfect plan.

What is your biggest rock? Realize that no one can survive this life without being belittled, abused, betrayed. But when such heavy rocks are put into the Master's hand, He will transform your pain into a priceless treasure.

The Master has His methods, and He uses far more than four when going about His work. But whatever the trial, whatever the test, whatever the turmoil, abrasives are actually *needed* so that you can reflect the incomparable character of Christ.

In this world, nothing has more worth!

And sure enough, when he came home from work that evening, he barked his customary question. With a pleasant smile, I responded, "I know where it is. Would you like for me to get it?"

I went to his bedroom and retrieved the address book. Dad seemed stunned and speechless by the servant heart and attitude he saw in me. And whatever the impact on him, it was empowering...and life-changing for me. From that time on, he was no longer my enemy and I was no longer his. I believe this was the fruit of my asking for forgiveness. It changed the dynamics of our relationship.

Asking forgiveness is a huge issue in relationships, and often never occurs because people never *feel* like it. Often the way people justify their offensive behavior toward others is by focusing on the guilt of others. This means that our offenders will want to blame us for our guilt in order to relieve themselves of their guilt. Then they do not feel the full weight of their own sin.

Can You End "The Blame Game"?

Picture a balancing scale. On the right side is guilt, on the left side is blame. As long as Dad could blame me for my negative attitude, then he would not feel the weight of his guilt. The scale is balanced—even if I am only 2 percent wrong—because Dad's focus is on what he can blame me for. Looking back, I can see how preposterous that 2 percent really was.

However, when we humbly ask forgiveness of our sin, our guilt is removed and our bag is emptied. And when our blame is lifted off one side of the scale, then the guilty feeling of our offender comes down heavily and quickly on the other side.

This is why, when we ask forgiveness for our sin, the Spirit of God can use our humble heart to bring *godly conviction* to our offender's heart. This means that asking forgiveness can bring an end to "the blame game."

After asking forgiveness of my father, I did not sense him

blaming me as he had previously. And although we never had a warm, affectionate relationship, I sought to find every opportunity to demonstrate honor and respect to him. I learned long ago that we can always be respectful to someone even if he or she is not respectful toward us.

Over time, however, I became aware that my father genuinely respected me as well.

My mother and father often sat in white rocking chairs on our front porch while entertaining guests, and one day an interesting exchange took place. A man tried to share the plan of salvation with my dad, who proceeded to quickly cut him off with, "If anybody's going to speak to me about spiritual things, it's going to be my daughter June."

On his eighty-sixth birthday I received that opportunity.

Dad seemingly was coming to grips with his own mortality as his health began to fail. He had polyps on his colon, for which he would not have surgery, because "all doctors want to do is cut on you." Later he was diagnosed with colon cancer.

To my surprise, Dad listened as I presented the plan of salvation at his bedside (see Appendix F on page 209). Then I asked him if he wanted to receive Jesus as his personal Lord and Savior. His response was, "Yes." So I led him in a simple prayer for salvation.

> *God, I want a real relationship with You. I admit that many times I've chosen to go my own way instead of Your way. Please forgive me for my sins. Jesus, thank You for dying on the cross to pay the penalty for my sins. Come into my life to be my Lord and my Savior. Take control of my life and make me the person You created me to be. In Your holy name I pray. Amen.*

I was totally amazed by my father's expression of humility—his seeming recognition of his need for the Savior. For the first time ever, he was willing to receive Jesus as his Lord and Savior!

I was eternally grateful for his response, but guarded. Was it real;

was it sincere? My mother confidently assured me that he would never have uttered such a prayer without it being authentic. My father, after all, had never been one to please or appease. Throughout the years, he had turned away many renowned Christian leaders who had sought to share the plan of salvation with him.

Something extraordinary occurred on that day. It's called a transplant—a heart transplant initiated by the Lord Himself. He said, "I will give you a new heart and put a new spirit in you; I will remove from you your heart of stone and give you a heart of flesh."[3]

It was blatantly apparent to me that the soil of my father's heart had, for years, been tilled primarily by Mother, who literally loved him into the kingdom of God, and also by my mother's amazing friends. These were godly women and men who showered grace upon grace on my dad, embodying agape love and emulating Christ.

My father died of colon cancer six months after receiving the greatest forgiveness of all: divine forgiveness. Not from me, not from Mother, but from Christ the Savior.

It's interesting—Dad used to say, "Christianity is a crutch." I used to say, "Dad will never change."

Thank God, we were both wrong.

My Prayer to Forgive My Offender

Lord Jesus,
thank You for caring about how much my heart has been hurt.
You know the pain I am feeling from (insert offense here).
Right now I release all that pain into Your hands.
Thank You, Lord, for dying on the cross for me and extending Your
forgiveness to me. As an act of my will, I choose to forgive (insert
person's name). *Right now, I take* (name) *off my emotional hook,*
and I place this person on Your hook. I refuse all thoughts of revenge.
I trust that in Your time and in Your way You will deal with my
offender as You see fit. And Lord, thank You for giving me Your
power to forgive so that I can be set free.
In Your precious name I pray. Amen.

Why Should We Get Rid of Unforgiveness?

The Unforgiving Heart Is...	The Unforgiving Heart Has...
Judgmental—focuses on the past wrongs that the offender committed	**Condemnation**—is intolerant of any present failures of the offender

Do not judge....Do not condemn....
Forgive, and you will be forgiven
(Luke 6:37).

Merciless—rehearses the reasons the offender does not deserve mercy	**Contempt**—looks down without mercy on the offender

Judgment without mercy will be shown to anyone who has not been merciful. Mercy triumphs over judgment!
(James 2:13).

Resentful—begrudges the successes of the offender	**Envy**—covets the accomplishments of the offender

Resentment kills a fool, and envy slays the simple (Job 5:2).

THE UNFORGIVING HEART IS...	THE UNFORGIVING HEART HAS...
Vengeful—rejoices when the offender experiences failure, difficulty, or hurt	**Retaliation**—desires to get even with the offender

Do not gloat when your enemy falls; when he stumbles, do not let your heart rejoice
(Proverbs 24:17).

Maligning—talks to others about the faults of the offender with the intent to hurt	**Slander**—shares unnecessary negatives about the offender

He who conceals his hatred has lying lips, and whoever spreads slander is a fool (Proverbs 10:18).

Prideful—elevates self above the offender, who is considered less deserving	**Haughtiness**—acts with arrogance toward the offender

Pride goes before destruction, a haughty spirit before a fall
(Proverbs 16:18).

Profane—verbally abusive toward the offender	**Bitterness**—harbors hostility toward the offender

Their mouths are full of cursing and bitterness
(Romans 3:14).

Complaining—quick to quarrel over personal choices, words, and deeds	**Resistance**—argues about any advice or constructive criticism regarding the offender

Do everything without complaining or arguing
(Philippians 2:14).

THE UNFORGIVING HEART IS...	THE UNFORGIVING HEART HAS...
Impatient—exhibits little patience while being easily provoked	*Annoyance*—feels easily irritated by the offender

A man's wisdom gives him patience;
it is to his glory to overlook an offense (Proverbs 19:11).

Bitter—feels weighed down with unresolved anger	*Negativity*—feels no joy and no approval concerning the offender

Each heart knows its own bitterness,
and no one else can share its joy
(Proverbs 14:10).

What Does the Forgiving Heart Look Like?

The fruit of the Spirit is love, joy, peace,
patience, kindness, goodness, faithfulness,
gentleness and self-control (Galatians 5:22-23).

The Forgiving Heart Is...

The Forgiving Heart Has...

Loving—does not keep a record of the bad things the offender has done

A loving spirit, allowing the possibility that the offender can change

Above all, love each other deeply,
because love covers over a multitude of sins (1 Peter 4:8).

Joyous—takes to heart the goodness of God and His sovereignty over all events in life, even the painful ones

A joyful awareness that God will use trials to bring triumph

I will continue to rejoice, for I know that through...the help given
by the Spirit of Jesus Christ, what has happened to me will turn out
for my deliverance (Philippians 1:18-19).

Peaceful—seeks to resolve any difficulty, hurt, or division and wants the offender to be right with God and to be blessed by Him

A peaceful demeanor that lowers the guard of the offender and paves the way for reconciliation

Peacemakers who sow in peace raise a harvest of righteousness
(James 3:18).

THE FORGIVING HEART IS...	THE FORGIVING HEART HAS...
Patient—accepts that the offender is not "fixed in cement" and could possibly change	**A patient commitment** that waits for the right day to deal with difficulties and the right time to talk about them

Love is patient (1 Corinthians 13:4).

Kind—looks for and acts in practical ways to express kind deeds and to meet needs	**A kind deed** on behalf of the offender that is unexpected, unforeseen, and unannounced

A kind man benefits himself,
but a cruel man brings trouble on himself
(Proverbs 11:17).

Good—holds to moral principles and purity even in the midst of controversy	**A good heart,** reflecting the highest moral character—the character of Christ

Give an answer.... do this with gentleness and respect, keeping a
clear conscience, so that those who speak maliciously against your
good behavior in Christ may be ashamed of their slander
(1 Peter 3:15-16).

Faithful—prays that those who have caused pain might have changed lives	**A faithful commitment** to pray for those who have been hurtful

Be joyful in hope, patient in affliction, faithful in prayer
(Romans 12:12).

THE FORGIVING HEART IS...	THE FORGIVING HEART HAS...
Gentle—takes into account the woundedness of the offender and responds to harshness with a calm gentleness	*A gentle response*, which understands that often "hurt people hurt people"

A gentle answer turns away wrath, but a harsh word stirs up anger (Proverbs 15:1).

Self-controlled—decides ahead of time how to respond when conflict arises	*A controlled response* that is Christlike so that, no matter what is said or done, there is a positive attitude toward the offender

Prepare your minds for action; be self-controlled (1 Peter 1:13).

The High Cost of Unforgiveness[1] vs. the High Reward of Forgiveness

Cast all your anxiety on him because he cares for you (1 Peter 5:7).

UNFORGIVENESS	FORGIVENESS
Unforgiveness blocks the door to salvation and God's forgiveness.	**Forgiveness** opens the door to salvation and God's forgiveness.

If you forgive men when they sin against you, your heavenly Father will also forgive you. But if you do not forgive men their sins, your Father will not forgive your sins (Matthew 6:14-15).

Unforgiveness allows a root of bitterness to grow.	**Forgiveness** keeps a root of bitterness from growing.

See to it that no one misses the grace of God and that no bitter root grows up to cause trouble and defile many (Hebrews 12:15).

Unforgiveness opens a door to Satan in our lives.	**Forgiveness** closes a door to Satan in our lives.

I have forgiven in the sight of Christ for your sake, in order that Satan might not outwit us. For we are not unaware of his schemes (2 Corinthians 2:10-11).

UNFORGIVENESS	FORGIVENESS
Unforgiveness causes us to walk in darkness.	**Forgiveness** brings us into the light.

Anyone who claims to be in the light but hates his brother is still in the darkness....whoever hates his brother is in the darkness and walks around in the darkness; he does not know where he is going, because the darkness has blinded him (1 John 2:9-11).

Unforgiveness is of Satan.	**Forgiveness** is of God.

If you harbor bitter envy and selfish ambition in your hearts.... Such "wisdom" does not come down from heaven but is earthly, unspiritual, of the devil (James 3:14-15).

Unforgiveness reflects a godless heart.	**Forgiveness** reflects a godly heart.

*The godless in heart harbor resentment;
even when he fetters them, they do not cry for help*
(Job 36:13).

Unforgiveness makes us captive to sin.	**Forgiveness** frees us.

I see that you are full of bitterness and captive to sin
(Acts 8:23).

Unforgiveness grieves the Spirit of God.	**Forgiveness** is empowered by the Spirit of God.

Do not grieve the Holy Spirit of God, with whom you were sealed for the day of redemption. Get rid of all bitterness, rage and anger, brawling and slander, along with every form of malice (Ephesians 4:30-31).

Appendix D

BREAKING SPIRITUAL STRONGHOLDS

IN A WAR, IF YOUR ENEMY GAINS A FOOTHOLD, that means your enemy has gained some of your ground. Your enemy has taken some of your territory. Now, with that foothold, your foe has a secure base from which there can be further advance.

If you have been hurt and, as a result, harbor anger in your heart, realize that your *unresolved anger* can become a foothold for the enemy. The Bible says,

> *"In your anger do not sin":*
> *Do not let the sun go down while you are still angry,*
> *and do not give the devil a foothold*
> (Ephesians 4:26-27).

How Spiritual Strongholds Develop

1. When you refuse to forgive your offender, you have *unresolved anger.*

2. Unresolved anger, in turn, allows Satan to set up a *stronghold in your mind.*

3. This stronghold is a *fortified place* from which *"flaming arrows of the evil one"* are flung (Ephesians 6:16).

203

4. These flaming arrows of accusation and unforgiveness can continue to burn in your heart and keep you *mentally captive to do the enemy's will.*

At this point you are engaged in spiritual warfare. In order to win the spiritual war, you need to recognize that the battle for freedom is fought in your mind. You need to take captive every thought of unforgiveness and release your unresolved anger to God. "You must rid yourselves of all such things as these: anger, rage, malice, slander, and filthy language from your lips" (Colossians 3:8).

The following "spiritual warfare prayer" will help you to honestly confront and release your anger to God and thereby rid yourself of such damaging habits.

Spiritual Warfare Prayer

Dear heavenly Father,

I don't want to be defeated in my life. Thank You that Jesus, who lives in me, is greater than Satan, who is in the world (read 1 John 4:4).

I know I have been bought with the price of Christ's blood, which was shed at Calvary. My body is not my own; it belongs to Christ (read 1 Corinthians 6:19-20).

Right now, I refuse all thoughts that are not from You (read 2 Corinthians 10:3-5).

I choose to forgive those who have hurt me, and I choose to release all my pain and anger into Your hands (read Colossians 3:13).

I resist Satan and all his power (read James 4:7).

As I stand in the full armor of God, I ask You to bind Satan and his demonic forces from having any influence over me (read Ephesians 6:11).

From now on, with the shield of faith, I will deflect and defeat every unforgiving thought that could defeat me (read Ephesians 6:16).

And I yield my life to Your plan and Your purpose (read Jeremiah 29:11).

In the holy name of Jesus I pray. Amen.

Appendix E

HOW CAN YOU FIND GOD'S FORGIVENESS?

1. God's purpose for you is *salvation*.

— What was God's motive in sending Christ to earth? To condemn you? No, to express His love for you by making salvation possible for you!

"God so loved the world that he gave his one and only Son, that whoever believes in him shall not perish but have eternal life. For God did not send his Son into the world to condemn the world, but to save the world through him" (John 3:16-17).

— What were Jesus' purposes in coming to earth? To make everything perfect and to remove all sin? No, His purposes were to forgive your sins, empower you to have victory over them, and enable you to live a fulfilled life!

"I [Jesus] have come that they may have life, and have it to the full" (John 10:10).

2. Your problem is *sin*.

— What exactly is sin? Sin is living independently of God's standard—knowing what is right, but choosing wrong.

"Anyone, then, who knows the good he ought to do and doesn't do it, sins" (James 4:17).

— What is the major consequence of sin? Spiritual death, and spiritual separation from God.

"The wages of sin is death, but the gift of God is eternal life in Christ Jesus our Lord." (Romans 6:23).

3. God's provision for you is the *Savior*.

— Can anything remove the penalty for sin? Yes. Jesus died on the cross to pay the penalty for your sins.

"God demonstrates his own love for us in this: While we were still sinners, Christ died for us" (Romans 5:8).

What is the solution to being separated from God? Belief in Jesus Christ as the only way to God the Father.

"Jesus answered, 'I am the way and the truth and the life. No one comes to the Father except through me'" (John 14:6).

4. Your part is *surrender*.

— Place your faith in (rely on) Jesus Christ as your personal Lord and Savior and reject your good works as a means of gaining God's approval.

"It is by grace you have been saved, through faith—and this not from yourselves, it is the gift of God—not by works, so that no one can boast" (Ephesians 2:8-9).

— Give Christ control of your life, entrusting yourself to Him.

"Jesus said to his disciples, 'If anyone would come after me, he must deny himself and take up his cross and follow me. For whoever wants to save his life will lose it, but whoever loses his life for me will find it. What good will it be for

a man if he gains the whole world, yet forfeits his soul?'"
(Matthew 16:24-26).

The moment you choose to believe in Christ—entrusting your
life to Him—He gives you His Spirit to live inside you. Then the
Spirit of Christ enables you to live the fulfilled life God has planned
for you, and He gives you His power to forgive others so that your
heart can begin to heal. If you want to be fully forgiven by God
and become the person God created you to be, you can tell Him in
a simple, heartfelt prayer like this:

Prayer of Salvation

God, I want a real relationship with You.
I admit that many times I've chosen to go my own way
instead of Your way. Please forgive me for my sins.
Jesus, thank You for dying on the cross to pay the
penalty for my sins. Come into my life to be my Lord and
my Savior. Give me Your power to practice forgiveness and
to love those who have wounded me.
Begin healing the hurts in my life with Your love and
make me the person You created me to be.
In Your holy name I pray. Amen.

God's Heart on Forgiveness

1. God commands that we forgive each other.

   "Be kind and compassionate to one another, forgiving each other, just as in Christ God forgave you" (Ephesians 4:32).

2. God wants us to forgive others because He has forgiven us.

   "Bear with each other and forgive whatever grievances you may have against one another. Forgive as the Lord forgave you" (Colossians 3:13).

3. God wants us to see unforgiveness as sin.

   "Anyone, then, who knows the good he ought to do and doesn't do it, sins" (James 4:17).

4. God wants us to get rid of unforgiveness and have a heart of mercy.

   "Blessed are the merciful, for they will be shown mercy" (Matthew 5:7).

5. God wants us to do our part to live in peace with everyone.

   "If it is possible, as far as it depends on you, live at peace with everyone" (Romans 12:18).

6. God wants us to overcome evil with good.

> "Do not be overcome by evil, but overcome evil with good" (Romans 12:21).

7. God wants us to be ministers of reconciliation.

> "God...reconciled us to himself through Christ and gave us the ministry of reconciliation: that God was reconciling the world to himself in Christ, not counting men's sins against them. And he has committed to us the message of reconciliation" (2 Corinthians 5:18-19).

HOW TO PRAY FOR THOSE WHO HURT YOU

"The fruit of the Spirit is love, joy, peace, patience, kindness, goodness, faithfulness, gentleness and self-control. Against such things there is no law" (Galatians 5:22-23).

Lord, I pray that (__NAME__) will be filled with *the fruit of love* by becoming fully aware of Your unconditional *love*—and in turn will be able to *love* others.

Lord, I pray that (__NAME__) will be filled with *the fruit of joy* because of experiencing Your steady *joy*—and in turn will radiate that inner *joy* to others.

Lord, I pray that (__NAME__) will be filled with *the fruit of peace*—Your inner *peace*—and in turn will have a *peace* that passes all understanding toward others.

Lord, I pray that (__NAME__) will be filled with *the fruit of patience* because of experiencing Your *patience*—and in turn will extend that same extraordinary *patience* to others.

Lord, I pray that (__NAME__) will be filled with *the fruit of kindness* because of experiencing Your *kindness*—and in turn will extend that same undeserved *kindness* to others.

Lord, I pray that (__NAME__) will be filled with *the fruit of goodness* because of experiencing the genuine *goodness* of Jesus—and in turn will reflect the moral *goodness* of Jesus before others.

Lord, I pray that (__NAME__) will be filled with *the fruit of faithfulness* because of realizing Your amazing *faithfulness*—and in turn will desire to be *faithful* to You, Your Word, and others.

Lord, I pray that (NAME) will be filled with *the fruit of gentleness* because of experiencing Your *gentleness*—and in turn will be able to be *gentle* with others.

Lord, I pray that (NAME) will be filled with *the fruit of self-control*—the *control of self* by Christ—and in turn will rely on Christ's *control* for enablement to break out of bondage and be an example before others.

In the name of Jesus I pray. Amen."

The wisdom that comes from heaven is first of all pure;
then peace-loving, considerate, submissive, full of mercy
and good fruit, impartial and sincere (James 3:17).

Appendix H

PRINCIPLES FOR FORGIVING MONETARY DEBT

The Bible is replete with teachings about money and debt. Questions about the handling of monetary debt can be especially thorny.

Principles for Borrowers

- Do everything within your power to avoid acquiring debts you cannot pay and to repay debts that you now owe.

- If you cannot repay the entire amount quickly, offer to make regular installments of *some amount*, even if it is very small.[1]

- God expects you to be a person of integrity—keeping your word, honoring your agreements, and fulfilling your obligations. Therefore, a person of integrity will *want* to repay legitimate debt.

- Even if a lender forgives your debt, should circumstances change and you later become able to begin repayment, offer to do so. If the lender restates the desire to dismiss the debt, then, with deepest gratitude, accept the generous gesture as a gift of grace.

Principles for Lenders

- If you've truly forgiven a debt, do not expect restitution, regardless of the borrower's ability or inability to repay.

- There are times when debt repayment is impossible. If adverse circumstances befall a borrower and render the person truly unable to repay a debt, then forgiving that person would be appropriate, and the default would not indicate a lack of integrity, but rather, a lack of ability.

- If you have forgiven a debt that the borrower later offers to repay, you retain the prerogative to accept the repayment, if offered, or you may reiterate your initial decision to dismiss the debt.

- The Israelites were required to cancel debts at the end of every seventh year. If you hold on to extended expectation of repayment and the debt is not repaid, you would likely become bitter. Such bitterness would be detrimental to all involved.[2]

NOTES

Chapter 1—"Sticks and Stones May Break My Bones..."

1. Proverbs 18:21.
2. 1 Corinthians 9:24.
3. Galatians 5:7.
4. Isaiah 40:31.

Chapter 2—The School of Hard Rocks

1. 1 John 2:9,11.

Chapter 3—"Stone Her! Stone Her!"

1. John 8:11 NKJV.
2. Psalm 18:2.
3. Proverbs 1:5.
4. Philippians 4:13.
5. Colossians 1:27.
6. 2 Peter 1:3-4 NKJV.
7. Romans 12:19.
8. Romans 4:7-8.
9. Psalm 103:10-12.
10. Matthew 11:28 NKJV.
11. Hebrews 12:1.

12. W.E. Vine, *Vine's Complete Expository Dictionary*, s.v. "Forgive, Forgave, Forgiveness."

13. Romans 12:17.

14. Proverbs 17:9.

Chapter 4—"What Father Gives His Child a Stone?"

1. Cathy Lunn-Grossman, "Americans' Image of God Varies," *USA Today*, September 11, 2006.

2. Matthew 7:9-11 ESV.

3. Psalm 103:10-12.

4. Micah 7:18-19.

5. Romans 8:1-2.

6. Luke 15:1-2 ESV.

7. Luke 15:32 ESV.

8. Romans 8:35,37-39.

9. Philippians 2:5-7.

10. Philippians 2:8.

11. Everett L. Worthington, *Forgiving and Reconciling: Bridges to Wholeness and Hope* (Downer's Grove, IL: InterVarsity Press, 2003), p. 49.

12. Exodus 32:28.

13. Acts 2:41.

14. John W. Reed, ed., *1100 Illustrations from the Writings of D.L. Moody for Teachers, Preachers, and Writers* (Grand Rapids: Baker Books, 1996), p. 172.

15. Psalm 100:5.

16. Matthew 18:21-22 NKJV.

17. Matthew 5:38-42.

18. 2 Corinthians 5:18.

19. Jeremiah 31:34.

20. Ron Lee Davis, *A Forgiving God in an Unforgiving World* (Grand Rapids: Zondervan Publishing House, 2003), pp. 3-4.

Chapter 5—Getting Rid of the Gravelly Remains

1. Micah 7:19.

2. Corrie ten Boom, *Tramp for the Lord* (New York: Berkley Publishing, 1978), pp. 55-57. Reprinted with permissions from *Guideposts* magazine. Copyright © 1972 by Guideposts, Carmel, New York 10512. All rights reserved. www.guidepostsmag.com.

3. Romans 2:14-15.

4. Deuteronomy 19:19-21.

5. Luke 6:36.

6. Psalm 51:1.

7. Luke 23:34.

8. Acts 10:43.

9. Isaiah 53:6.

10. 1 Peter 2:20-21,23.

11. Deuteronomy 32:35.

12. Luke 18:6-8.

13. Matthew 18:35.

14. Matthew 6:14-15.

15. See Acts 16:31.

16. 1 John 5:11.

17. Luke 6:37-38.

18. Matthew 6:14.

19. Hebrews 12:15.

20. 2 Corinthians 2:10-11.

21. 1 John 2:9-10.

22. Job 36:13.

23. Ephesians 4:30-31.

Chapter 6—Removing Hard Rocks of Resentment

1. John 3:16.

2. Romans 12:2.

3. Romans 8:1.

4. Romans 8:28.

5. Isaiah 48:10 ESV.

6. Malachi 3:2-3.

7. Genesis 37–45.

8. Genesis 39:21 ESV.

9. Genesis 40:8 ESV.

10. Genesis 45:5-8.

11. Genesis 45:5 ESV.

12. Genesis 45:7 8 ESV.

13. Proverbs 25:4.

14. Genesis 50:15.

15. Genesis 50:16.

16. Genesis 50:20 ESV.

17. Genesis 50:20.

18. Romans 8:28 ESV.

Chapter 7—Cutting the Bottom Out of the Bag

1. Isaiah 40:29 NKJV.

2. Proverbs 23:7 NKJV.

3. 2 Corinthians 10:5.

4. Michael E. McCullough, Steven J. Savage, Everett L. Worthington, *To Forgive Is Human: How to Put Your Past in the Past* (Downers Grove, IL: InterVarsity Press, 1997), p. 79.

5. Proverbs 24:17.

6. Matthew 6:12.

7. Robert Frost, *Our Heavenly Father* (Plainfield, NJ: Logos International, 1978), p. 63.

8. See Philippians 4:8.

9. Psalm 42:5; 42:11; 43:5.

10. 2 Corinthians 5:17 NKJV.

11. Matthew 6:12.

12. Proverbs 27:6 NKJV.

13. James 2:14.

14. Robert D. Enright, *Forgiveness Is a Choice: A Step-by-Step Process for Resolving Anger and Restoring Hope* (Washington, DC: APA Life Tools, American Psychological Association, 2001), p. 166.

15. Matthew 5:40-41.

Chapter 8—Rocks Aren't Removed Overnight

1. Ephesians 4:26.
2. John Bakeless, *The Journals of Lewis and Clark* (New York: Signet Classics, 2002), p. 51.
3. John 8:32.
4. Ephesians 5:11.
5. Proverbs 24:24.
6. Ecclesiastes 3:1,8.
7. Psalm 130:1.
8. Jeremiah 15:18.
9. Alexander Pope, *Essay on Criticism,* part 2 (Whitefish, MT: Kessinger Publishings, 2004), p. 19.
10. Mark 11:25.
11. 2 Peter 1:3.
12. Romans 12:19.
13. Matthew 18:21-22.
14. Philippians 3:13-14.
15. Richard Swenson, *A Minute of Margin* (Colorado Springs: NavPress, 2003), p. 103.
16. Philippians 2:1-2.
17. See Psalm 139:23-24.
18. Matthew 18:15.
19. See 2 Corinthians 7:10.
20. See Proverbs 12:19.
21. See Proverbs 10:17.
22. See Proverbs 4:23.
23. See Isaiah 43:18-19.
24. Psalm 146:7-8.

Chapter 9—Steering Clear of Stone Throwers

1. Amos 3:3.
2. 2 Corinthians 5:17-20.
3. Luke 15:21.
4. J.R.R. Tolkein, *The Hobbit* (Boston: Houghton Mifflin, 2001), p. 235.

5. Robert D. Enright, *Forgiveness Is a Choice* (Washington, DC: APA Life Tools, American Psychological Association, 2001), p. 30.

6. Romans 3:23.

7. C.S. Lewis, *The Four Loves* (New York: Harcourt Brace Jovanovich, 1960), p. 169.

8. Ephesians 4:15.

9. Galatians 1:10.

10. See Proverbs 28:13.

11. 2 Corinthians 7:10.

12. Luke 19:1-10 ESV.

13. Paul Meier, *Free to Forgive* (Nashville: Thomas Nelson Publishers, 1991), p. 58.

14. See 1 Corinthians 15:33.

Chapter 10—Breaking the Power of Your Pelter

1. Matthew 5:44 NKJV.

2. 1 Samuel 12:23.

3. Luke 1:37 NKJV.

4. 1 Peter 3:9-11.

5. Matthew 19:26.

6. Mark 9:23.

Chapter 11—Blindsided by a God-sized Boulder

1. "Excerpts from Amish killer's note," BBC News Online, http://newsbbc. co.uk/2/hi/Americas/5404714.stm.

2. 1 Peter 4:12 NKJV.

3. C.S. Lewis, *Mere Christianity* (New York: Scribners, 1997), p. 25.

4. Philip Yancey, *Where Is God When It Hurts?* (Grand Rapids: Zondervan Publishing House, 1990), p. 68.

5. Ibid., p. 18.

6. Job 23:10.

7. Romans 5:3-5.

8. Romans 8:28 NKJV.

9. Job 42:2,5-6.

10. Sally Cohn, "What the Amish Are Teaching America," CommonDreams. org; www.commondreams.org/views06/1006-33.htm.

Chapter 12—Buried Under Rocks of Regret

1. Micah 7:19.
2. Romans 8:1.
3. Robert South, *Sermons Preached Upon Several Occasions, Vol. 2* (Grand Rapids: Zondervan, 1997), p. 18.
4. 2 Corinthians 7:10.
5. Johann Christoph Arnold, *Why Forgive?* (Farmington, PA: Plough Publishing House, 2000), pp. 28-29.
6. 1 John 1:9.
7. Matthew 5:23-24.
8. Ephesians 1:7-8.
9. John 19:30.
10. Ephesians 4:22-23.
11. See Matthew 4:1-11.
12. John 8:44.
13. Psalm 103:10-12 NKJV.
14. Hebrews 10:36 ESV.
15. See Psalm 32:5.

Chapter 13—The Power of the Empty Bag

1. G.A. Pettit, "Forgiveness and Health," *In Context,* June 2000, http://www.context.org/ICLIB/IC39/Rijke.htm.
2. Brenda Goodman, "Forgiveness Is Good, Up to a Point," *Psychology Today,* January/February 2004; www. psychologytoday.com/articles.
3. See Ephesians 1:13-14.
4. See Galatians 5:22-23.
5. 1 Peter 4:8.
6. Philippians 1:18-19.
7. 2 Corinthians 13:11.
8. 1 Corinthians 13:4.
9. Zechariah 7:9 ESV.

10. 1 Peter 2:12.

11. Romans 12:12.

12. Proverbs 15:1.

13. 1 Peter 1:13.

14. This story is told in Lee Strobel and Gary Poole, *Experiencing the Passion of Jesus* (Grand Rapids, MI: Zondervan, 2004), pp. 75-76.

15. Martin Luther King Jr., *Strength to Love* (Philadelphia: Fortress Press, 1981), pp. 50, 56.

16. Romans 5:6-8.

17. Ellis Close, *Bone to Pick: Of Forgiveness, Reconciliation, and Revenge* (New York: Washington Square Press, 2004), p. 4.

Chapter 14—A Heart of Stone Finds Hope and Healing

1. Matthew 5:23-24.

2. Matthew 5:44.

3. Ezekiel 36:26.

Appendix C

1. Nieder and Thompson, *Forgive & Love Again* (Eugene, OR: Harvest House Publishers, 1991), pp. 47-51.

Appendix H

1. Romans 13:8.

2. Hebrews 12:15.